Gospel of John

NEW CENTURY VERSION

AUTHENTIC BIBLES

GOSPEL OF JOHN
New Century Version

ISBN: 1-86024-559-5

---

12 11 10 09 08 07 06 7 6 5 4 3 2 1
This edition published 2006 by Authentic Media, 9 Holdom Avenue, Bletchley, Milton Keynes, MK1 1QR and
129 Mobilization Drive, Waynesboro, GA 30830-4575, USA
www.authenticmedia.co.uk.
Authentic Media is a division of Send the Light Ltd.., a company limited by guarantee (registered charity no. 270162).
Print Management by Adare Carwin. Printed in Denmark by Nørhaven Paperback A/S.

Making Friends with Your Gospel of John

By Steve Chalke

At times the Bible can feel like the most hard-going, difficult, confusing and boring book that has ever been written.

The problem is that the Bible is very complicated.

☆ It isn't really a single book at all. The word "Bible" means "library" and that's exactly what it is – 66 books in all: 39 in the first section and 27 in the second.

☆ It was written by about 40 authors over a time period spanning more than 1000 years and it contains 750,000 words. And if that's not enough, the Old Testament was written in Hebrew and the New Testament in Greek!

So why bother? In a world where magazines, TV, radio, newspapers and other books bombard us with so many conflicting ideas about life, the Bible claims to be directly inspired by God himself – it's the creator's message to his world. If that's true it means that the Bible is in a completely different league from any other advice you can find. If the Bible is God's guidebook to life it makes sense to take it very, very seriously.

So, how do you make friends with the Bible and get the most out of reading it? Here are the ten do's and don'ts that have helped me.

1. Do use a modern translation. It's very important that you read a version which captures the depth of the original language at the same time as expressing its truth in a clear up to date way. That's where the *New Century Version* scores.

2. Don't rush – read slowly. Think about what you are reading. Quality comes before quantity. Read it more than once. You'll find that you'll notice all sorts of things you missed first time round. Remember that it's better to understand one verse than read a whole chapter and forget the lot!

3. Do pray first. Ask God to speak to you. You might just pray, "Help me, God, to discover you and your will as I read my Bible." After you've finished reading it pray and talk to God about the things that he has said to you or if you have found it hard to understand, be honest with him about it.

4. Don't use it as a lucky dip. Don't open it at random and expect some magic word or phrase to leap out and solve all your problems. If you do, you are almost bound to end up getting confused. And don't try and read it from cover to cover right away. As we've already said it is a big and complicated book. Like with all other guide-books the most sensible thing to do is to go to the issue you are thinking about at the time. Use one of the reading plans at the front of the Bible.

5. Do read it regularly. Just like food and exercise, "little and often" is best. If you can, set aside a short time every day to read a passage from the Bible and think it through. If your routine changes at the weekend, do something different then. Re-read what you have looked at during the week or talk it over with a friend. But remember that there is no right way to read the Bible. It's up to you to work out what suits you best.

6. Don't feel guilty if you miss a day. Why? Firstly because everyone does. So you aren't odd. Life doesn't always work out quite according to plan for anybody. Secondly, the important point isn't to have your daily dose of Bible once every 24 hours but to take in its message.

7. Do ask yourself lots of questions. It's your job to find out what it's really saying rather than inventing your own meanings. Only when you have got to grips with its original meaning can you go on to discover what it's saying to you now.

8. Don't be put off when you have a boring week or more! It happens to everyone and you are probably gaining far more than you realise – though of course that will be easier to see looking back than at the time. The secret is to be disciplined and just keep on going.

9. Do read it responsibly. Having a time when you read the Bible each day isn't an end in itself, it is only a means to an end – understanding more about Jesus Christ, your Lord and friend, boss and brother. The biggest question isn't how much we have read but about how much we have done about what we have read. Once having heard what God is saying about something we have a responsibility to act on it or to ignore it.

10. Don't be worried if you don't understand something. If you come across a difficult passage or anything that confuses you, get help. If you have a Bible commentary, concordance or Bible dictionary, check it out there. If you can't solve it ask your minister or a friend – someone that you trust to help you understand it.

Gospel of John

Christ Comes to the World

1 Before the world began, there was the Word.[1] The Word was with God, and the Word was God. 2He was with God in the beginning. 3All things were made through him. Nothing was made without him. 4In him there was life. That life was light for the people of the world. 5The Light shines in the darkness. And the darkness has not overpowered the Light.

6There was a man named John[2] who was sent by God. 7He came to tell people about the Light. Through him all people could hear about the Light and believe. 8John was not the Light, but he came to tell people about the Light. 9The true Light was coming into the world. The true Light gives light to all.

10The Word was in the world. The world was made through him, but the world did not know him. 11He came to the world that was his own. But his own people did not accept him. 12But some people did accept him. They believed in him. To them he gave the right to become children of God. 13They did not become his children in the human way. They were not born because of the desire or wish of some man. They were born of God.

[14]The Word became a man and lived among us. We saw his glory – the glory that belongs to the only Son of the Father. The Word was full of grace and truth. [15]John told about him. He said, "This is the One I was talking about. I said, 'The One who comes after me is greater than I am. He was living before me'."

[16]The Word was full of grace and truth. From him we all received more and more blessings. [17]The law was given through Moses, but grace and truth came through Jesus Christ. [18]No man has ever seen God, but God the only Son is very close to the Father.[3] And the Son has shown us what God is like.

John Tells People About Jesus

[19]The Jews in Jerusalem sent some priests and Levites to John.[2] The Jews sent them to ask, "Who are you?"

[20]John spoke freely and did not refuse to answer. He said clearly, "I am not the Christ."[d]

[21]So they asked him, "Then who are you? Are you Elijah?"[4]

He answered, "No, I am not Elijah."

Then they asked, "Are you the Prophet?"[5]

He answered, "No, I am not the Prophet."

[22]Then they said, "Who are you? Give us an answer to tell those who sent us. What do you say about yourself?"

[23]John told them in the words of the prophet Isaiah:

"I am the voice of a man
calling out in the desert:

'Make the road straight for the
Lord'."

Isaiah 40:3

[24]In the group of Jews who were sent, there were some Pharisees.[d] [25]They said to John: "You say you are not the Christ. You say you are not Elijah or the Prophet. Then why do you baptise people?"

[26]John answered, "I baptise people with water. But there is one here with you that you don't know. [27]He is the One who comes after me. I am not good enough to untie the strings of his sandals."

[28]This all happened at Bethany on the other side of the Jordan River. This is where John was baptising people.

[29]The next day John saw Jesus coming toward him. John said, "Look, the Lamb of God.[6] He takes away the sins of the world! [30]This is the One I was talking about. I said, 'A man will come after me, but he is greater than I am, because he was living before me'. [31]Even I did not know who he was. But I came baptising with water so that the people of Israel could know who he is."

[32-33]Then John said, "I did not know who the Christ was. But God sent me to baptise with water. And God told me, 'You will see the Spirit[d] come down and rest on a man. That man is the One who will baptise with the Holy Spirit'." John said, "I saw the Spirit come down from heaven. The Spirit looked like a dove and rested on him. [34]I have seen this happen. So I tell people: 'He is the Son of God'."

The First Followers of Jesus

[35]The next day John[2] was there again with two of his followers. [36]He saw Jesus walking by and said, "Look, the Lamb of God!"[6]

[37]The two followers heard John say this. So they followed Jesus. [38]Jesus turned and saw them following him. He asked, "What do you want?"

They said, "Rabbi, where are you staying?" ("Rabbi" means "Teacher".)

[39]Jesus answered, "Come with me and you will see." So the two men went with Jesus. They saw the place where Jesus was staying and stayed there with him that day. It was then about four o'clock.

[40]These two men followed Jesus after they heard about him from John. One of the men was Andrew. He was Simon Peter's brother. [41]The first thing Andrew did was to find his brother, Simon. He said to Simon, "We have found the Messiah." ("Messiah" means "Christ".[d])

[42]Then Andrew took Simon to Jesus. Jesus looked at Simon and said, "You are Simon son of John. You will be called Cephas." ("Cephas" means "Peter".[7])

[43]The next day Jesus decided to go to Galilee. He found Philip and said to him, "Follow me." [44]Philip was from the town of Bethsaida, where Andrew and Peter lived. [45]Philip found Nathanael and told him, "Remember that Moses wrote in the law about a man who was coming, and the prophets[d] also wrote about him. We have found him. He is Jesus, the son of Joseph. He is from Nazareth."

46But Nathanael said to Philip, "Nazareth! Can anything good come from Nazareth?"

Philip answered, "Come and see."

47Jesus saw Nathanael coming toward him. He said, "Here is truly a person of Israel. There is nothing false in him."

48Nathanael asked, "How do you know me?"

Jesus answered, "I saw you when you were under the fig tree. That was before Philip told you about me."

49Then Nathanael said to Jesus, "Teacher, you are the Son of God. You are the King of Israel."

50Jesus said to Nathanael, "You believe in me because I told you I saw you under the fig tree. But you will see greater things than that!" 51And Jesus said to them, "I tell you the truth. You will all see heaven open. You will see 'angels of God going up and coming down'[8] on the Son of Man."[d]

The Wedding at Cana

2 Two days later there was a wedding in the town of Cana in Galilee. Jesus' mother was there. 2Jesus and his followers were also invited to the wedding. 3When all the wine was gone, Jesus' mother said to him, "They have no more wine."

4Jesus answered, "Dear woman, why come to me? My time has not yet come."

5His mother said to the servants, "Do whatever he tells you to do."

6In that place there were six stone water jars. The Jews used jars like these in their washing ceremony.[9] Each jar held about 100 litres.

[7]Jesus said to the servants, "Fill the jars with water." So they filled the jars to the top.

[8]Then he said to them, "Now take some out and give it to the master of the feast."

So the servants took the water to the master. [9]When he tasted it, the water had become wine. He did not know where the wine came from. But the servants who brought the water knew. The master of the wedding called the bridegroom [10]and said to him, "People always serve the best wine first. Later, after the guests have been drinking a lot, they serve the cheaper wine. But you have saved the best wine till now."

[11]So in Cana of Galilee, Jesus did his first miracle.[d] There he showed his glory, and his followers believed in him.

Jesus in the Temple

[12]Then Jesus went to the town of Capernaum with his mother, brothers and his followers. They all stayed in Capernaum for a few days. [13]But it was almost time for the Jewish Passover[d] Feast. So Jesus went to Jerusalem. [14]In the Temple[d] he found men selling cattle, sheep, and doves. He saw others sitting at tables, exchanging money. [15]Jesus made a whip out of cords. Then he forced all these men, with the sheep and cattle, to leave the Temple. He turned over the tables and scattered the money of the men who were exchanging it. [16]Then he said to those who were selling pigeons, "Take these things out of here! Don't make my Father's house a place for buying and selling!"

[17]When this happened the followers remembered what was written in the Scriptures:[d] "My strong love for your Temple completely controls me."[10]

[18]The Jews said to Jesus, "Show us a miracle[d] for a sign. Prove that you have the right to do these things."

[19]Jesus answered, "Destroy this temple, and I will build it again in three days."

[20]The Jews answered, "Men worked 46 years to build this Temple! Do you really believe you can build it again in three days?"

[21](But the temple Jesus meant was his own body. [22]After Jesus was raised from death, his followers remembered that Jesus had said this. Then they believed the Scripture[d] and the words Jesus said.)

[23]Jesus was in Jerusalem for the Passover Feast. Many people believed in him because they saw the miracles he did. [24]But Jesus did not trust himself to them because he knew them all. [25]He did not need anyone to tell him about people. Jesus knew what was in a person's mind.

Jesus and Nicodemus

3 There was a man named Nicodemus who was one of the Pharisees.[d] He was an important Jewish leader. [2]One night Nicodemus came to Jesus. He said, "Teacher, we know that you are a teacher sent from God. No one can do the miracles[d] you do, unless God is with him."

[3]Jesus answered, "I tell you the truth. Unless a person is born again, he cannot be in God's kingdom."

[4]Nicodemus said, "But if a man is already old, how

can he be born again? He cannot enter his mother's body again. So how can he be born a second time?"

[5]But Jesus answered, "I tell you the truth. Unless a person is born from water and the Spirit,[d] he cannot enter God's kingdom. [6]A person's body is born from his human parents. But a person's spiritual life is born from the Spirit. [7]Don't be surprised when I tell you, 'You must all be born again'. [8]The wind blows where it wants to go. You hear the wind blow. But you don't know where the wind comes from or where it is going. It is the same with every person who is born from the Spirit."

[9]Nicodemus asked, "How can all this be possible?"

[10]Jesus said, "You are an important teacher in Israel. But you still don't understand these things? [11]I tell you the truth. We talk about what we know. We tell about what we have seen. But you don't accept what we tell you. [12]I have told you about things here on earth, but you do not believe me. So certainly you will not believe me if I tell you about the things of heaven! [13]The only one who has ever gone up to heaven is the One who came down from heaven – the Son of Man.[d]

[14]"Moses lifted up the snake in the desert.[11] It is the same with the Son of Man. The Son of Man must be lifted up too. [15]Then everyone who believes in him can have eternal life.

[16]"For God loved the world so much that he gave his only Son. God gave his Son so that whoever believes in him may not be lost, but have eternal life. [17]God did not send his Son into the world to judge the world guilty, but to save the world through him. [18]He who believes in

God's Son is not judged guilty. He who does not believe has already been judged guilty, because he has not believed in God's only Son. [19]People are judged by this fact: I am the Light from God that has come into the world. But men did not want light. They wanted darkness because they were doing evil things. [20]Everyone who does evil hates the light. He will not come to the light because it will show all the evil things he has done. [21]But he who follows the true way comes to the light. Then the light will show that the things he has done were done through God."

Jesus and John the Baptist

[22]After this, Jesus and his followers went into the area of Judea. There Jesus stayed with his followers and baptised people. [23]John was also baptising in Aenon, near Salim, because there was plenty of water there. People were going there to be baptised. [24](This was before John was put into prison.)

[25]Some of John's followers had an argument with a Jew about religious washing.[9] [26]So they came to John and said, "Teacher, remember the man who was with you on the other side of the Jordan River, the one you spoke about? He is baptising, and everyone is going to him."

[27]John answered, "A man can get only what God gives him. [28]You yourselves heard me say, 'I am not the Christ.[d] I am only the one God sent to prepare the way for him'. [29]The bride belongs only to the bridegroom. The friend who helps the bridegroom waits and listens for him. He is glad when he hears the bridegroom's

voice. That is the same pleasure I have. And my time of joy is now here. [30]He must become greater. And I must become less important.

The One Who Comes from Heaven

[31]"The One who comes from above is greater than all. He who is from the earth belongs to the earth and talks about things on the earth. But the One who comes from heaven is greater than all. [32]He tells what he has seen and heard, but no one accepts what he says. [33]The person who accepts what he says has proved that God is true. [34]God sent him, and he tells the things that God says. God gives him the Spirit[d] fully. [35]The Father loves the Son and has given him power over everything. [36]He who believes in the Son has eternal life. But he who does not obey the Son will never have that life. God's anger stays with him."

Jesus and a Samaritan Woman

4 [1]The Pharisees[d] heard that Jesus was getting and baptising more followers than John. [2](But really Jesus himself did not baptise people. His followers did the baptising.) Jesus knew that the Pharisees had heard about him. [3]So he left Judea and went back to Galilee. [4]On the way he had to go through the country of Samaria.

[5]In Samaria Jesus came to the town called Sychar. This town is near the field that Jacob gave to his son Joseph. [6]Jacob's well was there. Jesus was tired from his long trip, so he sat down beside the well. It was about six o'clock in the evening. [7]A Samaritan[d] woman came to the

well to get some water. Jesus said to her, "Please give me a drink." [8](This happened while Jesus' followers were in town buying some food.)

[9]The woman said, "I am surprised that you ask me for a drink. You are a Jew and I am a Samaritan." (Jews are not friends with Samaritans.[12])

[10]Jesus said, "You don't know what God gives. And you don't know who asked you for a drink. If you knew, you would have asked me, and I would have given you living water."

[11]The woman said, "Sir, where will you get that living water? The well is very deep, and you have nothing to get water with. [12]Are you greater than Jacob, our father? Jacob is the one who gave us this well. He drank from it himself. Also, his sons and flocks drank from this well."

[13]Jesus answered, "Every person who drinks this water will be thirsty again. [14]But whoever drinks the water I give will never be thirsty again. The water I give will become a spring of water flowing inside him. It will give him eternal life."

[15]The woman said to him, "Sir, give me this water. Then I will never be thirsty again. And I will not have to come back here to get more water."

[16]Jesus told her, "Go and get your husband and come back here."

[17]The woman answered, "But I have no husband."

Jesus said to her, "You are right to say you have no husband. [18]Really you have had five husbands. But the man you live with now is not your husband. You told the truth."

[19]The woman said, "Sir, I can see that you are a prophet.[d] [20]Our fathers worshipped on this mountain. But you Jews say that Jerusalem is the place where people must worship."

[21]Jesus said, "Believe me, woman. The time is coming when you will not have to be in Jerusalem or on this mountain to worship the Father. [22]You Samaritans worship what you don't understand. We Jews understand what we worship. Salvation comes from the Jews. [23]The time is coming when the true worshippers will worship the Father in spirit and truth. That time is now here. And these are the kinds of worshippers the Father wants. [24]God is spirit. Those who worship God must worship in spirit and truth."

[25]The woman said, "I know that the Messiah is coming." (Messiah is the One called Christ.[d]) "When the Messiah comes, he will explain everything to us."

[26]Then Jesus said, "He is talking to you now. I am he."

[27]Just then his followers came back from town. They were surprised because they saw Jesus talking with a woman. But none of them asked, "What do you want?" or "Why are you talking with her?"

[28]Then the woman left her water jar and went back to town. She said to the people, [29] "A man told me everything I have ever done. Come and see him. Perhaps he is the Christ!" [30]So the people left the town and went to see Jesus.

[31]While the woman was away, the followers were begging him, "Teacher, eat something!"

[32]But Jesus answered, "I have food to eat that you know nothing about."

[33]So the followers asked themselves, "Has somebody already brought Jesus some food?"

[34]Jesus said, "My food is to do what the One who sent me wants me to do. My food is to finish the work that he gave me to do. [35]You say, 'Four more months to wait before we gather the grain'. But I tell you, open your eyes. Look at the fields that are ready for harvesting now. [36]Even now, the one who harvests the crop is being paid. He is gathering crops for eternal life. So now the one who plants can be happy along with the one who harvests. [37]It is true when we say, 'One person plants, but another harvests the crop'. [38]I sent you to harvest a crop that you did not work for. Others did the work, and you get the profit from their work."[13]

[39]Many of the Samaritans in that town believed in Jesus. They believed because of what the woman said: "He told me everything I have ever done." [40]The Samaritans came to Jesus and begged him to stay with them. So he stayed there two days. [41]Many more believed because of the things he said.

[42]They said to the woman, "First we believed in Jesus because of what you told us. But now we believe because we heard him ourselves. We know that this man really is the Saviour of the world."

Jesus Heals an Officer's Son

[43]Two days later, Jesus left and went to Galilee. [44](Jesus had said before that a prophet*d* is not respected in his own country.) [45]When Jesus arrived in Galilee, the people there welcomed him. They had had seen all the

things he did at the Passover[d] Feast in Jerusalem. They had been at the Passover Feast, too.

46Jesus went to visit Cana in Galilee again. This is where Jesus had changed the water into wine. One of the king's important officers lived in the city of Capernaum. This man's son was sick. 47The man heard that Jesus had come from Judea and was now in Galilee. He went to Jesus and begged him to come to Capernaum and heal his son. His son was almost dead. 48Jesus said to him, "You people must see signs and miracles[d] before you will believe in me."

49The officer said, "Sir, come before my child dies."

50Jesus answered, "Go. Your son will live."

The man believed what Jesus told him and went home. 51On the way the man's servants came and met him. They told him, "Your son is well."

52The man asked, "What time did my son begin to get well?"

They answered, "It was about one o'clock yesterday when the fever left him."

53The father knew that one o'clock was the exact time that Jesus had said, "Your son will live." So the man and all the people of his house believed in Jesus.

54That was the second miracle that Jesus did after coming from Judea to Galilee.

Jesus Heals a Man at a Pool

5 Later Jesus went to Jerusalem for a special Jewish feast. 2In Jerusalem there is a pool with five covered porches. In the Jewish language[14] it is called

Bethesda.[15] This pool is near the Sheep Gate. [3]Many sick people were lying on the porches beside the pool. Some were blind, some were crippled, and some were paralysed.[16] [5]There was a man lying there who had been sick for 38 years. [6]Jesus saw the man and knew that he had been sick for a very long time. So Jesus asked him, "Do you want to be well?"

[7]The sick man answered, "Sir, there is no one to help me get into the pool when the water starts moving. I try to be the first one into the water. But when I try, someone else always goes in before I can."

[8]Then Jesus said, "Stand up. Pick up your mat and walk." [9]And immediately the man was well. He picked up his mat and began to walk.

The day all this happened was a Sabbath[d] day. [10]So the Jews said to the man who had been healed, "Today is the Sabbath. It is against our law for you to carry your mat on the Sabbath day."

[11]But he answered, "The man who made me well told me, 'Pick up your mat and walk'."

[12]Then they asked him, "Who is the man who told you to pick up your mat and walk?"

[13]But the man who had been healed did not know who it was. There were many people in that place, and Jesus had left.

[14]Later, Jesus found the man at the Temple.[d] Jesus said to him, "See, you are well now. But stop sinning or something worse may happen to you!"

[15]Then the man left and went back to the Jews. He told them that Jesus was the one who had made him well.

[16]Jesus was doing this on the Sabbath day. So the Jews began to do bad things to him. [17]But Jesus said to them, "My Father never stops working. And so I work, too."

[18]This made the Jews try harder to kill him. They said, "First Jesus was breaking the law about the Sabbath day. Then he said that God is his own Father! He is making himself equal with God!"

Jesus Has God's Authority

[19]But Jesus said, "I tell you the truth. The Son can do nothing alone. The Son does only what he sees his Father doing. The Son does whatever the Father does. [20]The Father loves the Son, and the Father shows the Son all the things he himself does. But the Father will show the Son greater things than this to do. Then you will all be amazed. [21]The Father raises the dead and gives them life. In the same way, the Son gives life to those he wants to. [22]Also, the Father judges no one. But the Father has given the Son power to do all the judging. [23]God did this so that all people will respect the Son the same way they respect the Father. He who does not respect the Son does not respect the Father. The Father is the One who sent the Son.

[24]"I tell you the truth. Whoever hears what I say and believes in the One who sent me has eternal life. He will not be judged guilty. He has already left death and has entered into life. [25]I tell you the truth. The time is coming and is already here when the dead will hear the voice of the Son of God. And those who hear will have life. [26]Life comes from the Father himself. So the Father

has allowed the Son to give life. 27And the Father has given the Son the power to judge because he is the Son of Man.[d] 28Don't be surprised at this. A time is coming when all who are dead and in their graves will hear his voice. 29Then they will come out of their graves. Those who did good will rise and have life for ever. But those who did evil will rise to be judged guilty.

Jesus Is God's Son

30"I can do nothing alone. I judge only the way I am told, so my judgement is right. I don't try to please myself. I try to please the One who sent me.

31"If I tell people about myself, then they will not accept what I say about myself. 32But there is another who tells about me. And I know that the things he says about me are true.

33"You have sent men to John.[2] And he has told you about the truth. 34But I don't need a man to tell about me. I tell you this so that you can be saved. 35John was like a burning and shining lamp. And you were happy to enjoy his light for a while.

36"But I have a proof about myself that is greater than that of John. The things I do are my proof. These are the things my Father gave me to do. They show that the Father sent me. 37And the Father who sent me has given proof about me himself. You have never heard his voice. You have never seen what he looks like. 38His teaching does not live in you because you don't believe in the One that the Father sent. 39You carefully study the Scriptures[d] because you think that they give you eternal life. Those are the same Scriptures that tell about me! [40]But you refuse to come to me to have that life.

[41]"I don't want praise from men. [42]But I know you – I know that you don't have God's love in you. [43]I have come from my Father – I speak for him. But you don't accept me. But when another person comes, speaking only for himself, you will accept him. [44]You like to have praise from each other. But you never try to get the praise that comes from the only God. So how can you believe? [45] Don't think that I will stand before the Father and say that you are wrong. Moses is the one who says that you are wrong. And he is the one that you hoped would save you. [46]If you really believed Moses, you would believe me because Moses wrote about me. [47]But you don't believe what Moses wrote. So how can you believe what I say?"

More than 5,000 People Fed

6 After this, Jesus went across Lake Galilee (or, Lake Tiberias). [2]Many people followed him because they saw the miracles[d] he did to heal the sick. [3]Jesus went up on a hill and there sat down with his followers. [4]It was almost the time for the Jewish Passover[d] Feast.

[5]Jesus looked up and saw a large crowd coming toward him. He said to Philip, "Where can we buy bread for all these people to eat?" [6](Jesus asked Philip this question to test him. Jesus already knew what he planned to do.)

[7]Philip answered, "We would all have to work a month to buy enough bread for each person here to have only a little piece."

[8]Another follower there was Andrew. He was Simon Peter's brother. Andrew said, [9]"Here is a boy with five loaves of barley bread and two little fish. But that is not enough for so many people."

[10]Jesus said, "Tell the people to sit down." This was a very grassy place. There were about 5,000 men who sat down there. [11]Then Jesus took the loaves of bread. He thanked God for the bread and gave it to the people who were sitting there. He did the same with the fish. He gave them as much as they wanted.

[12]They all had enough to eat. When they had finished, Jesus said to his followers, "Gather the pieces of fish and bread that were not eaten. Don't waste anything." [13]So they gathered up the pieces that were left. They filled 12 large baskets with the pieces that were left of the five barley loaves.

[14]The people saw this miracle that Jesus did. They said, "He must truly be the Prophet[5] who is coming into the world."

[15]Jesus knew that the people planned to come and take him by force and make him their king. So he left and went into the hills alone.

Jesus Walks on the Water

[16]That evening Jesus' followers went down to Lake Galilee. [17]It was dark now and Jesus had not yet come to them. The followers got into a boat and started across the lake to Capernaum. [18]By now a strong wind was blowing, and the waves on the lake were getting bigger. [19]They rowed the boat about four or five kilometres.

Then they saw Jesus walking on the water, coming toward the boat. The followers were afraid. [20]But Jesus said to them, "Don't be afraid. It is I." [21]Then they were glad to take him into the boat. At once the boat came to land at the place where they wanted to go.

The People Seek Jesus

[22]The next day came. Some people had stayed on the other side of the lake. They knew that Jesus had not gone in the boat with his followers but that they had left without him. And they knew that only one boat had been there. [23]But then some boats came from Tiberias. They landed near the place where the people had eaten the bread after the Lord had given thanks. [24]The people saw that Jesus and his followers were not there now. So they got into boats and went to Capernaum. They wanted to find Jesus.

Jesus, the Bread of Life

[25]The people found Jesus on the other side of the lake. They asked him, "Teacher, when did you come here?"

[26]Jesus answered, "Are you looking for me because you saw me do miracles?[d] No! I tell you the truth. You are looking for me because you ate the bread and were satisfied. [27]Earthly food spoils and ruins. So don't work to get that kind of food. But work to get the food that stays good always and gives you eternal life. The Son of Man[d] will give you that food. God the Father has shown that he is with the Son of Man."

[28]The people asked Jesus, "What are the things God wants us to do?"

[29]Jesus answered, "The work God wants you to do is this: to believe in the One that God sent."

[30]So the people asked, "What miracle will you do? If we can see a miracle, then we will believe you. What will you do? [31]Our fathers ate the manna[d] in the desert. This is written in the Scriptures:[d] 'God gave them bread from heaven to eat'."[17]

[32]Jesus said, "I tell you the truth. Moses was not the one who gave you bread from heaven. But my Father gives you the true bread from heaven. [33]God's bread is the One who comes down from heaven and gives life to the world."

[34]The people said, "Sir, give us this bread always."

[35]Then Jesus said, "I am the bread that gives life. He who comes to me will never be hungry. He who believes in me will never be thirsty. [36]But as I told you before, you have seen me, and still you don't believe. [37]The Father gives me my people. Every one of them will come to me, and I will always accept them. [38]I came down from heaven to do what God wants me to do. I did not come to do what I want to do. [39]I must not lose even one of those that God has given me, but I must raise them up on the last day. This is what the One who sent me wants me to do. [40]Everyone who sees the Son and believes in him has eternal life. I will raise him up on the last day. This is what my Father wants."

[41]The Jews began to complain about Jesus. They complained because he said, "I am the bread that comes

down from heaven." 42The Jews said, "This is Jesus. We know his father and mother. He is only Joseph's son. How can he say, 'I came down from heaven'?"

43But Jesus answered, "Stop complaining to each other. 44The Father is the One who sent me. No one can come to me unless the Father draws him to me. And I will raise him up on the last day. 45It is written in the prophets,[d] 'God will teach all the people'.[18] Everyone who listens to the Father and learns from him comes to me. 46No one has seen the Father except the One who is from God. Only he has seen the Father. 47I tell you the truth. He who believes has eternal life. 48I am the bread that gives life. 49Your ancestors ate the manna in the desert. But still they died. 50Here is the bread that comes down from heaven. If anyone eats this bread, he will never die. 51I am the living bread that came down from heaven. If anyone eats this bread, he will live for ever. This bread is my flesh. I will give my flesh so that the people in the world may have life."

52Then the Jews began to argue among themselves. They said, "How can this man give us his flesh to eat?"

53Jesus said, "I tell you the truth. You must eat the flesh of the Son of Man. And you must drink his blood. If you don't do this, then you won't have real life in you. 54He who eats my flesh and drinks my blood has eternal life. I will raise him up on the last day. 55My flesh is true food. My blood is true drink. 56Whoever eats my flesh and drinks my blood lives in me, and I live in him. 57The Father sent me. The Father lives, and I live because of the Father. So he who eats me will live because of me.

[58]I am not like the bread our ancestors ate. They ate that bread, but still they died. I am the bread that came down from heaven. He who eats this bread will live for ever." [59]Jesus said all these things while he was teaching in the synagogue[d] in Capernaum.

The Words of Eternal Life

[60]The followers of Jesus heard this. Many of them said, "This teaching is hard. Who can accept it?"

[61]Jesus knew that his followers were complaining about this. So he said, "Does this teaching bother you? [62]If so will it also bother you to see the Son of Man[d] going back to the place where he came from? [63]It is not the flesh that gives a person life. It is the spirit that gives life. The words I told you are spirit, and so they give life. [64]But some of you don't believe." (Jesus knew who did not believe. He knew this from the beginning. And he knew who would turn against him.) [65]Jesus said, "That is the reason I said, 'If the Father does not let a person come to me, then he cannot come'."

[66]After Jesus said this, many of his followers left him. They stopped following him.

[67]Jesus asked the 12 followers, "Do you want to leave, too?"

[68]Simon Peter answered Jesus, "Lord, where would we go? You have the words that give eternal life. [69]We believe in you. We know that you are the Holy One from God."

[70]Then Jesus answered, "I chose all 12 of you. But one of you is a devil."

[71]Jesus was talking about Judas, the son of Simon Iscariot. Judas was one of the 12. But later he was going to turn against Jesus.

Jesus and His Brothers

7 After this, Jesus travelled around Galilee. He did not want to travel in Judea, because the Jews there wanted to kill him. [2]It was time for the Jewish Feast[d] of Shelters. [3]So Jesus' brothers said to him, "You should leave here and go to Judea. Then your followers there can see the miracles[d] you do. [4]Anyone who wants to be well known does not hide what he does. If you are doing these things, show yourself to the world." [5](Even Jesus' brothers did not believe in him.)

[6]Jesus said to his brothers, "The right time for me has not yet come. But any time is right for you. [7]The world cannot hate you. But it hates me, because I tell about the evil things it does. [8]So you go to the feast. I will not go now. The right time for me has not yet come." [9]After saying this, Jesus stayed in Galilee.

[10]So Jesus' brothers left to go to the feast. When they had gone, Jesus went, too. But he did not let people see him. [11]At the feast the Jews were looking for him. They said, "Where is that man?"

[12]There was a large crowd of people there. Many of them were whispering to each other about Jesus. Some said, "He is a good man."

Others said, "No, he fools the people." [13]But no one was brave enough to talk about Jesus openly. They were afraid of the Jews.

Jesus Teaches at the Feast

[14]The feast was about half over. Then Jesus went to the Temple[d] and began to teach. [15]The Jews were amazed. They said, "This man has never studied in school. How did he learn so much?"

[16]Jesus answered, "The things I teach are not my own. My teaching comes from him who sent me. [17]If anyone chooses to do what God wants, then he will know that my teaching comes from God. He will know that this teaching is not my own. [18]He who teaches his own ideas is trying to get honour for himself. But he who tries to bring honour to the one who sent him – that person speaks the truth. There is nothing false in him. [19]Moses gave you the law,[19] but none of you obey that law. Why are you trying to kill me?"

[20]The people answered, "A demon[d] has come into you. We are not trying to kill you."

[21]Jesus said to them, "I did one miracle,[d] and you are all amazed. [22]Moses gave you the law about circumcision.[d] (But really Moses did not give you circumcision. Circumcision came from our ancestors.) And yet you circumcise a baby on a Sabbath[d] day. [23]This shows that a baby can be circumcised on a Sabbath day to obey the law of Moses. So why are you angry at me for healing a person's whole body on the Sabbath day? [24]Stop judging by the way things look! Be fair, and judge by what is really right."

Is Jesus the Christ?

[25]Then some of the people who lived in Jerusalem said, "This is the man they are trying to kill. [26]But he is

teaching where everyone can see and hear him. And no one is trying to stop him. Perhaps the leaders have decided that he really is the Christ.[d] [27]But we know where this man is from. And when the real Christ comes, no one will know where he comes from."

[28]Jesus was still teaching in the Temple.[d] He cried out, "Yes, you know me, and you know where I am from. But I have not come by my own authority. I was sent by the One who is true. You don't know him. [29]But I know him. I am from him, and he sent me."

[30]When Jesus said this, the people tried to take him. But no one was able to touch him. It was not yet the right time. [31]But many of the people believed in Jesus. They said, "When the Christ comes, will he do more miracles[d] than this man has done?"

Some Leaders Try to Arrest Jesus

[32]The Pharisees[d] heard the crowd whispering these things about Jesus. So the leading priests and the Pharisees sent some Temple[d] guards to arrest him. [33]Then Jesus said, "I will be with you a little while longer. Then I will go back to the One who sent me. [34]You will look for me, but you will not find me. And you cannot come where I am."

[35]The Jews said to each other, "Where will this man go so we cannot find him? Will he go to the Greek cities where our people live? Will he teach the Greek people there? [36]This man says, 'You will look for me but you will not find me'. He also says, 'You cannot come where I am'. What does this mean?"

Jesus Talks About the Spirit

37The last day of the feast came. It was the most important day. On that day Jesus stood up and said in a loud voice, "If anyone is thirsty, let him come to me and drink. 38If a person believes in me, rivers of living water will flow out from his heart. This is what the Scripture[d] says." 39Jesus was talking about the Holy Spirit.[d] The Spirit had not yet been given because Jesus had not yet been raised to glory. But later, those who believed in Jesus would receive the Spirit.

The People Argue About Jesus

40The people heard these things that Jesus said. Some of them said, "This man really is the Prophet."[5]

41Others said, "He is the Christ."[d] Still others said, "The Christ will not come from Galilee. 42The Scripture[d] says that the Christ will come from David's family. And the Scripture says that the Christ will come from Bethlehem, the town where David lived." 43So the people did not agree with each other about Jesus. 44Some of them wanted to arrest him, but no one was able to touch him.

The Leaders Won't Believe

45The Temple[d] guards went back to the leading priests and the Pharisees.[d] The priests and the Pharisees asked, "Why didn't you bring Jesus?"

46The Temple guards answered, "The things he says are greater than the words of any man!"

47The Pharisees answered, "So Jesus has fooled you too! 48Have any of the leaders or the Pharisees believed in him? No! 49But those people, who know nothing about the law, are under God's curse!"

50But Nicodemus was there in that group. He was the one who had gone to see Jesus before.[20] Nicodemus said, 51"Our law does not judge a man without hearing him. We cannot judge him until we know what he has done."

52They answered, "Are you from Galilee too? Study the Scriptures.[d] You will learn that no prophet[d] comes from Galilee."

53And everyone left and went home.[21]

The Woman Caught in Adultery

8 Jesus went to the Mount of Olives.[d] 2But early in the morning he went back to the Temple.[d] All the people came to Jesus, and he sat and taught them. 3The teachers of the law and the Pharisees[d] brought a woman there. She had been caught in adultery.[d] They forced the woman to stand before the people. 4They said to Jesus, "Teacher, this woman was caught having sexual relations with a man who is not her husband. 5The law of Moses commands that we kill with stones every woman who does this. What do you say we should do?" 6They were asking this to trick Jesus so that they could have some charge against him.

But Jesus knelt down and started writing on the ground with his finger. 7They continued to ask Jesus their question. So he stood up and said, "Is there anyone here who has never sinned? The person without sin can throw the first stone at this woman." [8]Then Jesus knelt down again and wrote on the ground.

[9]Those who heard Jesus began to leave one by one. The older men left first, and then the others. Jesus was left there alone with the woman. She was standing before him. [10]Jesus stood up again and asked her, "Woman, all of those people have gone. Has no one judged you guilty?"

[11]She answered, "No one has judged me, sir."

Then Jesus said, "So I don't judge you either. You may go now, but don't sin again."

Jesus Is the Light of the World

[12]Later, Jesus talked to the people again. He said, "I am the light of the world. The person who follows me will never live in darkness. He will have the light that gives life."

[13]But the Pharisees[d] said to Jesus, "When you talk about yourself, you are the only one to say these things are true. We cannot accept these things you say."

[14]Jesus answered, "Yes, I am saying these things about myself, but they are true. I know where I came from. And I know where I am going. You don't know where I came from or where I am going. [15]You judge me the way you would judge any man. I don't judge anyone. [16]But if I judge, my judging is true. When I judge, I am not alone. The Father who sent me is with me. [17]Your own law says that when two witnesses say the same thing, then you must accept what they say. [18]I am one of

the witnesses who speaks about myself. And the Father who sent me is my other witness."

[19]They asked, "Where is your father?"

Jesus answered, "You don't know me or my Father. But if you knew me, then you would know my Father, too." [20]Jesus said these things while he was teaching in the Temple.[d] He was near the place where the money that the people give is kept. But no one arrested him. The right time for Jesus had not yet come.

The People Misunderstand Jesus

[21]Again, Jesus said to the people, "I will leave you. You will look for me, but you will die in your sins. You cannot come where I am going."

[22]So the Jews asked, "Will Jesus kill himself? Is that why he said, 'You cannot come where I am going'?"

[23]But Jesus said, "You people are from here below, but I am from above. You belong to this world, but I don't belong to this world. [24]So I told you that you would die in your sins. Yes, you will die in your sins if you don't believe that I am he."

[25]They asked, "Then who are you?"

Jesus answered, "I am what I have told you from the beginning. [26]I have many things to say about you and to judge you for. But I tell people only the things I have heard from the One who sent me. And he speaks the truth."

[27]The people did not understand that Jesus was talking to them about the Father. [28]So Jesus said to them, "You will lift up the Son of Man.[d] Then you will

know that I am he. You will know that these things I do are not by my own authority. You will know that I say only what the Father has taught me. [29]The One who sent me is with me. I always do what is pleasing to him. So he has not left me alone." [30]While Jesus was saying these things, many people believed in him.

Freedom from Sin

[31]So Jesus said to the Jews who believed in him, "If you continue to obey my teaching, you are truly my followers. [32]Then you will know the truth. And the truth will make you free."

[33]The Jews answered, "We are Abraham's children. And we have never been slaves. So why do you say that we will be free?"

[34]Jesus answered, "I tell you the truth. Everyone who lives in sin is a slave to sin. [35]A slave does not stay with a family for ever, but a son belongs to the family for ever. [36]So if the Son makes you free, then you will be truly free. [37]I know you are Abraham's children. But you want to kill me because you don't accept my teaching. [38]I am telling you what my Father has shown me. But you do what your father has told you."

[39]They answered, "Our father is Abraham."

Jesus said, "If you were really Abraham's children, you would do the things that Abraham did. [40]I am a man who has told you the truth which I heard from God. But you are trying to kill me. Abraham did nothing like that. [41]So you are doing the things that your own father did."

But the Jews said, "We are not like children who never

knew who their father was. God is our Father. He is the only Father we have."

[42]Jesus said to them, "If God were really your Father, you would love me. I came from God and now I am here. I did not come by my own authority. God sent me. [43]You don't understand what I say because you cannot accept my teaching. [44]Your father is the devil. You belong to him and want to do what he wants. He was a murderer from the beginning. He was against the truth, for there is no truth in him. He is a liar, and he is like the lies he tells. He is the father of lies. [45]But I speak the truth. That is why you don't believe me. [46]Can any of you prove that I am guilty of sin? If I am telling the truth, why don't you believe me? [47]He who belongs to God accepts what God says. But you don't accept what God says, because you don't belong to God."

Jesus and Abraham

[48]The Jews answered, "We say you are a Samaritan![d] We say a demon[d] has come into you. Are we not right?"

[49]Jesus answered, "I have no demon in me. I give honour to my Father, but you dishonour me. [50]I am not trying to get honour for myself. There is One who wants this honour for me, and he is the judge. [51]I tell you the truth. If anyone obeys my teaching, he will never die."

[52]The Jews said to Jesus, "Now we know that you have a demon in you! Even Abraham and the prophets[d] died. But you say, 'Whoever obeys my teaching will never die'. [53]Do you think that you are greater than our father

Abraham? Abraham died. And the prophets died, too. Who do you think you are?"

[54]Jesus answered, "If I give honour to myself, that honour is worth nothing. The One who gives me honour is my Father. And you say that he is your God. [55]But you don't really know him. I know him. If I said I did not know him, then I would be a liar as you are liars. But I do know him, and I obey what he says. [56]Your father Abraham was very happy that he would see my day. He saw that day and was glad."

[57]The Jews said to him, "What? You have seen Abraham! You are not even 50 years old!"

[58]Jesus answered, "I tell you the truth. Before Abraham was born, I am!" [59]When Jesus said this, the people picked up stones to throw at him. But Jesus hid himself, and then he left the Temple.[d]

Jesus Heals a Man Born Blind

9 As Jesus was walking along, he saw a man who had been born blind. [2]His followers asked him, "Teacher, whose sin caused this man to be born blind – his own sin or his parents' sin?"

[3]Jesus answered, "It is not this man's sin or his parents' sin that caused him be blind. This man was born blind so that God's power could be shown in him. [4]While it is day time, we must continue doing the work of the One who sent me. The night is coming. And no one can work at night. [5]While I am in the world, I am the light of the world."

[6]After Jesus said this, he spat on the ground and

made some mud with it. He put the mud on the man's eyes. [7]Then he told the man, "Go and wash in the Pool of Siloam." (Siloam means Sent.) So the man went to the pool. He washed and came back. And he was able to see.

[8]Some people had seen this man begging before. They and the man's neighbours said, "Look! Is this the same man who always sits and begs?"

[9]Some said, "Yes! He is the one." But others said, "No, he's not the same man. He only looks like him."

So the man himself said, "I am the man."

[10]They asked, "What happened? How did you get your sight?"

[11]He answered, "The man named Jesus made some mud and put it on my eyes. Then he told me to go to Siloam and wash. So I went and washed and came back seeing."

[12]They asked him, "Where is this man?"

The man answered, "I don't know."

Pharisees Question the Healing

[13]Then the people took to the Pharisees[d] the man who had been blind. [14]The day Jesus had made mud and healed his eyes was a Sabbath[d] day. [15]So now the Pharisees asked the man, "How did you get your sight?"

He answered, "He put mud on my eyes. I washed, and now I can see."

[16]Some of the Pharisees were saying, "This man does not keep the Sabbath day. He is not from God!"

Others said, "But a man who is a sinner can't do miracles[d] like these." So they could not agree with each other.

[17]They asked the man again, "What do you say about him? It was your eyes he opened."

The man answered, "He is a prophet."[d]

[18]The Jews did not believe that he had been blind and could now see again. So they sent for the man's parents [19]and asked them, "Is this your son? You say that he was born blind. Then how does he see now?"

[20]His parents answered, "We know that this is our son, and we know that he was born blind. [21]But we don't know how he can see now. We don't know who opened his eyes. Ask him. He is old enough to answer for himself." [22]His parents said this because they were afraid of the Jews. The Jews had already decided that anyone who said that Jesus was the Christ[d] would be put out of the synagogue.[d] [23]That is why his parents said, "He is old enough. Ask him."

[24]So for the second time, the Jewish leaders called the man who had been blind. They said, "You should give God the glory by telling the truth. We know that this man is a sinner."

[25]He answered, "I don't know if he is a sinner. But one thing I do know. I was blind, and now I can see."

[26]The Jewish leaders asked, "What did he do to you? How did he make you see again?"

[27]He answered, "I have already told you that. But you would not listen to me. Why do you want to hear it again? Do you want to become his followers, too?"

[28]Then they insulted him and said, "You are his follower. We are followers of Moses. [29]We know that God spoke to Moses. But we don't even know where this man comes from!"

[30]The man answered, "This is a very strange thing. You don't know where he comes from, and yet he opened my eyes. [31]We all know that God does not listen to sinners. But God listens to anyone who worships and obeys him. [32]Nobody has ever heard of anyone giving sight to a man born blind. [33]If this man was not from God, he could do nothing."

[34]They answered, "You were born full of sin! Are you trying to teach us?" And they threw the man out.

Spiritual Blindness

[35]Jesus heard that they had thrown him out. So Jesus found him and said, "Do you believe in the Son of Man?"[d]

[36]He asked, "Who is the Son of Man, sir? Tell me, so I can believe in him!"

[37]Jesus said to him, "You have already seen him. The Son of Man is the one talking with you now."

[38]He said, "Yes, Lord, I believe!" Then the man bowed and worshipped Jesus.

[39]Jesus said, "I came into this world that the world could be judged. I came so that the blind[22] could see and so that those who see will become blind."

[40]Some of the Pharisees[d] were near Jesus. When they heard him say this, they asked, "What? Are you saying that we are blind, too?"

[41]Jesus said, "If you were really blind, you would not be guilty of sin. But now that you say you can see, your guilt remains."

The Shepherd and His Sheep

10 Jesus said, "I tell you the truth. The man who does not enter the sheep fold by the door, but climbs in some other way, is a thief and a robber. [2]The one who enters by the door is the shepherd of the sheep. [3]The man who guards the door opens it for him. And the sheep listen to the voice of the shepherd. He calls his own sheep, using their names, and he leads them out. [4]He brings all of his sheep out. Then he goes ahead of them and leads them. They follow him because they know his voice. [5]But they will never follow a stranger. They will run away from him because they don't know his voice." [6]Jesus told the people this story, but they did not understand what it meant.

Jesus Is the Good Shepherd

[7]So Jesus said again, "I tell you the truth. I am the door for the sheep. [8]All the people who came before me were thieves and robbers. The sheep did not listen to them. [9]I am the door. The person who enters through me will be saved. He will be able to come in and go out and find pasture. [10]A thief comes to steal and kill and destroy. But I came to give life – life in all its fullness.

[11]"I am the good shepherd. The good shepherd gives his life for the sheep. [12]The worker who is paid to keep

the sheep is different from the shepherd who owns them. So when the worker sees a wolf coming, he runs away and leaves the sheep alone. Then the wolf attacks the sheep and scatters them. [13]The man runs away because he is only a paid worker. He does not really care for the sheep.

[14–15]"I am the good shepherd. I know my sheep, as the Father knows me. And my sheep know me, as I know the Father. I give my life for the sheep. [16]I have other sheep that are not in this flock here. I must bring them also. They will listen to my voice, and there will be one flock and one shepherd. [17]The Father loves me because I give my life. I give my life so that I can take it back again. [18]No one takes it away from me. I give my own life freely. I have the right to give my life, and I have the right to take it back. This is what my Father commanded me to do."

[19]Again the Jews did not agree with each other because of these words Jesus said. [20]Many of them said, "A demon[d] has come into him and made him mad. Why listen to him?"

[21]But others said, "A man who is mad with a demon does not say things like this. Can a demon open the eyes of the blind?"

[22]The time came for the Feast[d] of Dedication at Jerusalem. This was during the winter. [23]Jesus was walking in the Temple[d] in Solomon's Porch.[d] [24]The Jews gathered around him and said, "How long will you make us wonder about you? If you are the Christ,[d] then tell us plainly."

Jesus Is the Son of God

[25]Jesus answered, "I have told you already, but you did not believe. I do miracles[d] in my Father's name. Those miracles show who I am. [26]But you don't believe because you are not my sheep. [27]My sheep listen to my voice. I know them, and they follow me. [28]I give them eternal life, and they will never die. And no person can steal them out of my hand. [29]My Father gave my sheep to me. He is greater than all, and no person can steal my sheep out of my Father's hand. [30]The Father and I are one."

[31]Again the Jews picked up stones to kill Jesus. [32]But Jesus said to them, "I have done many good works from the Father. Which of these good works are you killing me for?"

[33]The Jews answered, "We are not killing you for any good work you did. But you say things that are against God. You are only a man, but you say you are the same as God!"

[34]Jesus answered, "It is written in your law that God said, 'I have said you are gods!'[23] [35]This scripture[d] called those people gods, the people who received God's message. And Scripture is always true. [36]So why do you say that I speak against God because I said, 'I am God's Son'? I am the one God chose and sent into the world. [37]If I don't do what my Father does, then don't believe me. [38]But if I do what my Father does, even though you don't believe in me, believe what I do. Then you will know and understand that the Father is in me and I am in the Father."

39The Jews tried to take Jesus again, but he escaped from them.

40Then Jesus went back across the Jordan River to the place where John[2] had first baptised. Jesus stayed there, 41and many people came to him. They said, "John never did a miracle. But everything John said about this man is true." 42And in that place many believed in Jesus.

The Death of Lazarus

11 There was a man named Lazarus who was sick. He lived in the town of Bethany, where Mary and her sister Martha lived. 2Mary is the woman who later put perfume on the Lord and wiped his feet with her hair. Mary's brother was Lazarus, the man who was now sick. 3So Mary and Martha sent someone to tell Jesus, "Lord, the one you love is sick."

4When Jesus heard this he said, "This sickness will not end in death. It is for the glory of God. This has happened to bring glory to the Son of God." 5Jesus loved Martha and her sister and Lazarus. 6But when he heard that Lazarus was sick, he stayed where he was for two more days. 7Then Jesus said to his followers, "Let us go back to Judea."

8The followers said, "But Teacher, the Jews there tried to kill you with stones. That was only a short time ago. Now you want to go back there?"

9Jesus answered, "Are there not 12 hours in the day? If anyone walks in the daylight, he will not stumble because he can see by this world's light. 10But if anyone walks at night he stumbles because there is no light to help him see."

[11]After Jesus said this, he added, "Our friend Lazarus has fallen asleep. But I am going there to wake him."

[12]The followers said, "But Lord, if he can sleep, he will get well."

[13]Jesus meant that Lazarus was dead. But Jesus' followers thought that he meant Lazarus was really sleeping. [14]So then Jesus said plainly, "Lazarus is dead. [15]And I am glad for your sakes that I was not there so that you may believe. But let us go to him now."

[16]Then Thomas (the one called Didymus) said to the other followers, "Let us go, too. We will die with him."

Jesus in Bethany

[17]Jesus arrived in Bethany. There he learned that Lazarus had already been dead and in the tomb for four days. [18]Bethany was about three kilometres from Jerusalem. [19]Many Jews had come there to comfort Martha and Mary about their brother.

[20]Martha heard that Jesus was coming, and she went out to meet him. But Mary stayed at home. [21]Martha said to Jesus, "Lord, if you had been here, my brother would not have died. [22]But I know that even now God will give you anything you ask."

[23]Jesus said, "Your brother will rise and live again."

[24]Martha answered, "I know that he will rise and live again in the resurrection**[24]** on the last day."

[25]Jesus said to her, "I am the resurrection and the life. He who believes in me will have life even if he dies. [26]And he who lives and believes in me will never die. Martha, do you believe this?"

[27]Martha answered, "Yes, Lord. I believe that you are the Christ,[d] the Son of God. You are the One who was coming to the world."

Jesus Cries

[28]After Martha said this, she went back to her sister Mary. She talked to Mary alone. Martha said, "The Teacher is here and he is asking for you." [29]When Mary heard this, she got up quickly and went to Jesus. [30]Jesus had not yet come into the town. He was still at the place where Martha had met him. [31]The Jews were with Mary in the house, comforting her. They saw Mary stand and leave quickly. They followed her, thinking that she was going to the tomb to cry there. [32]But Mary went to the place where Jesus was. When she saw him, she fell at his feet and said, "Lord, if you had been here, my brother would not have died."

[33]Jesus saw that Mary was crying and that the Jews who came with her were crying, too. Jesus felt very sad in his heart and was deeply troubled. [34]He asked, "Where did you bury him?"

"Come and see, Lord," they said.

[35]Jesus cried.

[36]So the Jews said, "See how much he loved him."

[37]But some of them said, "If Jesus healed the eyes of the blind man, why didn't he keep Lazarus from dying?"

Jesus Raises Lazarus

[38]Again Jesus felt very sad in his heart. He came to the tomb. The tomb was a cave with a large stone covering the entrance. [39]Jesus said, "Move the stone away."

Martha said, "But, Lord, it has been four days since he died. There will be a bad smell." Martha was the sister of the dead man.

[40]Then Jesus said to her, "Didn't I tell you that if you believed, you would see the glory of God?"

[41]So they moved the stone away from the entrance. Then Jesus looked up and said, "Father, I thank you that you heard me. [42]I know that you always hear me. But I said these things because of the people here around me. I want them to believe that you sent me." [43]After Jesus said this, he cried out in a loud voice, "Lazarus, come out!" [44]The dead man came out. His hands and feet were wrapped with pieces of cloth, and he had a cloth around his face.

Jesus said to them, "Take the cloth off him and let him go."

The Leaders Plan to Kill Jesus

[45]There were many Jews who had come to visit Mary. They saw what Jesus did. And many of them believed in him. [46]But some of the Jews went to the Pharisees.[d] They told the Pharisees what Jesus had done. [47]Then the leading priests and Pharisees called a meeting of the Jewish council. They asked, "What should we do? This man is doing many miracles.[d] [48]If we let him continue doing these things, everyone will believe in him. Then the Romans will come and take away our Temple[d] and our nation."

[49]One of the men there was Caiaphas. He was the high priest that year. Caiaphas said, "You people know

nothing! [50]It is better for one man to die for the people than for the whole nation to be destroyed. But you don't realise this."

[51]Caiaphas did not think of this himself. He was high priest that year. So he was really prophesying[d] that Jesus would die for the Jewish nation [52]and for God's scattered children. This would bring them all together and make them one.

[53]That day the Jewish leaders started planning to kill Jesus. [54]So Jesus no longer travelled openly among the Jews. He left there and went to a place near the desert. He went to a town called Ephraim and stayed there with his followers.

[55]It was almost time for the Jewish Passover[d] Feast. Many from the country went up to Jerusalem before the Passover. They went to do the special things to make themselves pure. [56]The people looked for Jesus. They stood in the Temple and were asking each other, "Is he coming to the Feast? What do you think?" [57]But the leading priests and the Pharisees had given orders about Jesus. They said that if anyone knew where Jesus was, he must tell them. Then they could arrest Jesus.

Jesus with Friends in Bethany

12 Six days before the Passover[d] Feast, Jesus went to Bethany, where Lazarus lived. (Lazarus is the man Jesus raised from death.) [2]There they had a dinner for Jesus. Martha served the food. Lazarus was one of the people eating with Jesus. [3]Mary brought in half a litre of very expensive perfume made from pure nard.[d]

She poured the perfume on Jesus' feet, and then she wiped his feet with her hair. And the sweet smell from the perfume filled the whole house.

[4]Judas Iscariot, one of Jesus' followers, was there. (He was the one who would later turn against Jesus.) Judas said, [5]"This perfume was worth 300 silver coins.[25] It should have been sold and the money given to the poor." [6]But Judas did not really care about the poor. He said this because he was a thief. He was the one who kept the money box, and he often stole money from it.

[7]Jesus answered, "Leave her alone. It was right for her to save this perfume for today – the day for me to be prepared for burial. [8]The poor will always be with you, but you will not always have me."

The Plot Against Lazarus

[9]A large crowd of Jews heard that Jesus was in Bethany. So they went there to see not only Jesus but also Lazarus. Lazarus was the one Jesus raised from death. [10]So the leading priests made plans to kill Lazarus, too. [11]Because of Lazarus many Jews were leaving them and believing in Jesus.

Jesus Enters Jerusalem

[12]The next day a great crowd in Jerusalem heard that Jesus was coming there. These were the people who had come to the Passover[d] Feast. [13]They took branches of palm trees and went out to meet Jesus. They shouted,

"Praise[26] God!
God bless the One who comes in the name of the Lord!
God bless the King of Israel!"

Psalm 118: 25–26

[14]Jesus found a colt and sat on it. This was as the Scripture[d] says,

[15]"Don't be afraid, people of Jerusalem!
Your king is coming.
He is sitting on the colt of a donkey."

Zechariah 9:9

[16]The followers of Jesus did not understand this at first. But after Jesus was raised to glory, they remembered that this had been written about him. And they remembered that they had done these things to him.

People Tell About Jesus

[17]There had been many people with Jesus when he raised Lazarus from death and told him to come out of the tomb. Now they were telling others about what Jesus did. [18]Many people went out to meet Jesus, because they had heard about this miracle.[d] [19]So the Pharisees[d] said to each other, "You can see that nothing is going right for us. Look! The whole world is following him."

Jesus Talks About His Death

[20]There were some Greek people, too, who came to Jerusalem to worship at the Passover[d] Feast. [21]They

went to Philip. (Philip was from Bethsaida, in Galilee.) They said, "Sir, we would like to see Jesus." [22]Philip told Andrew. Then Andrew and Philip told Jesus.

[23]Jesus said to them, "The time has come for the Son of Man[d] to receive his glory. [24]I tell you the truth. A grain of wheat must fall to the ground and die. Then it makes many seeds. But if it never dies, it remains only a single seed. [25]The person who loves his life will give up true life. But the person who hates his life in this world will keep true life for ever. [26]Whoever serves me must follow me. Then my servant will be with me everywhere I am. My Father will honour anyone who serves me.

[27]"Now I am very troubled. What should I say? Should I say, 'Father, save me from this time'? No, I came to this time so that I could suffer. [28]Father, bring glory to your name!"

Then a voice came from heaven, "I have brought glory to it, and I will do it again."

[29]The crowd standing there heard the voice. They said it was thunder.

But others said, "An angel has spoken to him."

[30]Jesus said, "That voice was for you, not for me. [31]Now is the time for the world to be judged. Now the ruler of this world will be thrown down. [32]I will be lifted up from the earth. And when this happens, I will draw all people toward me." [33]Jesus said this to show how he would die.

[34]The crowd said, "We have heard from the law that the Christ[d] will live for ever. So why do you say, 'The Son of Man must be lifted up'? Who is this 'Son of Man'?"

[35]Then Jesus said, "The light will be with you for a little longer. So walk while you have the light. Then the darkness will not catch you. He who walks in the darkness does not know where he is going. [36]So believe in the light while you still have it. Then you will become sons of light." When Jesus had said this, he left and hid himself from them.

Some Don't Believe in Jesus

[37]Though Jesus had done many miracles[d] before the people, they still did not believe in him. [38]This was to make clear the full meaning of what Isaiah the prophet[d] said:

> "Lord, who believed the things we told them?
> Who has seen the Lord's power?"
>
> *Isaiah* 53:1

[39]This is why the people could not believe: Isaiah also said,

> [40]"He has blinded their eyes.
> He has closed their minds.
> This is so that they will not see with their eyes
> nor understand in their minds.
> This is so they will not
> come back to me and be forgiven."
>
> *Isaiah* 6:10

[41]Isaiah said this because he saw Jesus' glory and spoke about him.

[42]But many people believed in Jesus, even many of the Jewish leaders. But because of the Pharisees,[d] they did not say that they believed in him. They were afraid that they would be put out of the synagogue.[d] [43]They loved praise from men more than praise from God.

[44]Then Jesus cried out, "He who believes in me is really believing in the One who sent me. [45]He who sees me sees the One who sent me. [46]I have come as light into the world. I came so that whoever believes in me would not stay in darkness.

[47]"If anyone hears my words and does not obey them, I do not judge him. For I did not come to judge the world, but to save the world. [48]There is a judge for the one who refuses to believe in me and does not accept my words. The word I have taught will be his judge on the last day. [49]The things I taught were not from myself. The Father who sent me told me what to say and what to teach. [50]And I know that eternal life comes from what the Father commands. So whatever I say is what the Father told me to say."

Jesus Washes His Followers' Feet

13 It was almost time for the Jewish Passover[d] Feast. Jesus knew that it was time for him to leave this world and go back to the Father. He had always loved those who were his own in the world, and he loved them all the way to the end.

[2]Jesus and his followers were at the evening meal. The devil had already persuaded Judas Iscariot to turn against Jesus. (Judas was the son of Simon.) [3]Jesus

knew that the Father had given him power over everything. He also knew that he had come from God and was going back to God. [4]So during the meal Jesus stood up and took off his outer clothing. Taking a towel, he wrapped it around his waist. [5]Then he poured water into a bowl and began to wash the followers' feet. He dried them with the towel that was wrapped around him.

[6]Jesus came to Simon Peter. But Peter said to Jesus, "Lord, are you going to wash my feet?"

[7]Jesus answered, "You don't understand what I am doing now. But you will understand later."

[8]Peter said, "No! You will never wash my feet."

Jesus answered, "If I don't wash your feet, then you are not one of my people."

[9]Simon Peter answered, "Lord, after you wash my feet, wash my hands and my head, too!"

[10]Jesus said, "After a person has had a bath, his whole body is clean. He needs only to wash his feet. And you men are clean,[d] but not all of you." [11]Jesus knew who would turn against him. That is why Jesus said, "Not all of you are clean."

[12]When he had finished washing their feet, he put on his clothes and sat down again. Jesus asked, "Do you understand what I have just done for you? [13]You call me 'Teacher' and 'Lord'. And this is right, because that is what I am. [14]I, your Lord and Teacher, have washed your feet. So you also should wash each other's feet. [15]I did this as an example for you. So you should do as I have done for you. [16]I tell you the truth. A servant is not

greater than his master. A messenger is not greater than the one who sent him. [17]If you know these things, you will be happy if you do them.

[18]"I am not talking about all of you. I know those I have chosen. But what the Scripture[d] said must happen: 'The man who ate at my table has now turned against me'.[27] [19]I am telling you this now before it happens. Then when it happens you will believe that I am he. [20]I tell you the truth. Whoever accepts anyone I send also accepts me. And whoever accepts me also accepts the One who sent me."

Jesus Talks About His Death

[21]After Jesus said this, he was very troubled. He said openly, "I tell you the truth. One of you will turn against me."

[22]The followers all looked at each other. They did not know whom Jesus was talking about. [23]One of the followers was sitting[28] next to Jesus. This was the follower Jesus loved. [24]Simon Peter made signs to him to ask Jesus who it was that he was talking about.

[25]That follower leaned closer to Jesus and asked, "Lord, who is it that will turn against you?"

[26]Jesus answered, "I will dip this bread into the dish. The man I give it to is the man who will turn against me." So Jesus took a piece of bread. He dipped it and gave it to Judas Iscariot, the son of Simon. [27]As soon as Judas took the bread, Satan entered him. Jesus said to Judas, "The thing that you will do – do it quickly!" [28]None of the men at the table understood why Jesus said this to Judas.

[29]He was the one who kept the money box. So some of the followers thought that Jesus was telling Judas to buy what was needed for the feast. Or they thought that Jesus wanted Judas to give something to the poor.

[30]Judas accepted the bread Jesus gave him and immediately went out. It was night.

[31]When Judas was gone, Jesus said, "Now the Son of Man[d] receives his glory. And God receives glory through him. [32]If God receives glory through him, then God will give glory to the Son through himself. And God will give him glory quickly."

[33]Jesus said, "My children, I will be with you only a little longer. You will look for me. And what I told the Jews, I tell you now: where I am going you cannot come.

[34]"I give you a new command: love each other. You must love each other as I have loved you. [35]All people will know that you are my followers if you love each other."

Peter Will Say He Doesn't Know Jesus

[36]Simon Peter asked Jesus, "Lord, where are you going?"

Jesus answered, "Where I am going you cannot follow now. But you will follow later."

[37]Peter asked, "Lord, why can't I follow you now? I am ready to die for you!"

[38]Jesus answered, "Will you really die for me? I tell you the truth. Before the cock crows, you will say three times that you don't know me."

Jesus Comforts His Followers

14 Jesus said, "Don't let your hearts be troubled. Trust in God. And trust in me. [2]There are many rooms in my Father's house. I would not tell you this if it were not true. I am going there to prepare a place for you. [3]After I go and prepare a place for you, I will come back. Then I will take you to be with me so that you may be where I am. [4]You know the way to the place where I am going."

[5]Thomas said to Jesus, "Lord, we don't know where you are going. So how can we know the way?"

[6]Jesus answered, "I am the way. And I am the truth and the life. The only way to the Father is through me. [7]If you really knew me, then you would know my Father, too. But now you do know him, and you have seen him."

[8]Philip said to him, "Lord, show us the Father. That is all we need."

[9]Jesus answered, "I have been with you a long time now. Do you still not know me, Philip? He who has seen me has seen the Father. So why do you say, 'Show us the Father'? [10]Don't you believe that I am in the Father and the Father is in me? The words I say to you don't come from me. The Father lives in me, and he is doing his own work. [11]Believe me when I say that I am in the Father and the Father is in me. Or believe because of the miracles[d] I have done. [12]I tell you the truth. He who believes in me will do the same things that I do. He will do even greater things than these because I am going to the Father. [13]And if you ask for anything in my name, I will do it for you. Then the Father's glory will be shown

through the Son. [14]If you ask me for anything in my name, I will do it.

The Promise of the Holy Spirit

[15]"If you love me, you will do the things I command. [16]I will ask the Father, and he will give you another Helper.[29] He will give you this Helper to be with you for ever. [17]The Helper is the Spirit[d] of truth. The world cannot accept him because it does not see him or know him. But you know him. He lives with you and he will be in you.

[18]"I will not leave you all alone like orphans. I will come back to you. [19]In a little while the world will not see me any more, but you will see me. Because I live, you will live, too. [20]On that day you will know that I am in my Father. You will know that you are in me and I am in you. [21]He who knows my commands and obeys them is the one who loves me. And my Father will love him who loves me. I will love him and will show myself to him."

[22]Then Judas (not Judas Iscariot) said, "But, Lord, why do you plan to show yourself to us, but not to the world?"

[23]Jesus answered, "If anyone loves me, then he will obey my teaching. My Father will love him, and we will come to him and make our home with him. [24]He who does not love me does not obey my teaching. This teaching that you hear is not really mine. It is from my Father, who sent me.

[25]"I have told you all these things while I am with you.

[26]But the Helper will teach you everything. He will cause you to remember all the things I told you. This Helper is the Holy Spirit whom the Father will send in my name.

[27]"I leave you peace. My peace I give you. I do not give it to you as the world does. So don't let your hearts be troubled. Don't be afraid. [28]You heard me say to you, 'I am going, but I am coming back to you'. If you loved me, you should be happy that I am going back to the Father because he is greater than I am. [29]I have told you this now, before it happens. Then when it happens, you will believe. [30]I will not talk with you much longer. The ruler of this world is coming. He has no power over me. [31]But the world must know that I love the Father. So I do exactly what the Father told me to do.

"Come now, let us go."

Jesus Is Like a Vine

15 "I am the true vine; my Father is the gardener. [2]He cuts off every branch of mine that does not produce fruit. And he trims and cleans every branch that produces fruit so that it will produce even more fruit. [3]You are already clean[d] because of the words I have spoken to you. [4]Remain in me, and I will remain in you. No branch can produce fruit alone. It must remain in the vine. It is the same with you. You cannot produce fruit alone. You must remain in me.

[5]"I am the vine, and you are the branches. If a person remains in me and I remain in him, then he produces much fruit. But without me he can do nothing. [6]If anyone does not remain in me, then he is like a branch that is

thrown away. That branch dies. People pick up dead branches, throw them into the fire, and burn them. [7]Remain in me and follow my teachings. If you do this, then you can ask for anything you want, and it will be given to you. [8]You should produce much fruit and show that you are my followers. This brings glory to my Father. [9]I loved you as the Father loved me. Now remain in my love. [10]I have obeyed my Father's commands, and I remain in his love. In the same way, if you obey my commands, you will remain in my love. [11]I have told you these things so that you can have the same joy I have. I want your joy to be the fullest joy.

[12]"This is my command: love each other as I have loved you. [13]The greatest love a person can show is to die for his friends. [14]You are my friends if you do what I command you. [15]I don't call you servants now. A servant does not know what his master is doing. But now I call you friends because I have made known to you everything I heard from my Father. [16]You did not choose me; I chose you. And I gave you this work, to go and produce fruit. I want you to produce fruit that will last. Then the Father will give you anything you ask for in my name. [17]This is my command: love each other.

Jesus Warns His Followers

[18]"If the world hates you, remember that it hated me first. [19]If you belonged to the world, then it would love you as it loves its own. But I have chosen you out of the world. So you don't belong to it. That is why the world hates you. [20]Remember what I told you: a servant is not

greater than his master. If people did wrong to me, they will do wrong to you, too. And if they obeyed my teaching, they will obey yours, too. [21]They will do all this to you because of me. They don't know the One who sent me. [22]If I had not come and spoken to them, they would not be guilty of sin. But now they have no excuse for their sin. [23]He who hates me also hates my Father. [24]I did works among them that no one else has ever done. If I had not done those works, they would not be guilty of sin. But now they have seen what I did, and yet they have hated both me and my Father. [25]But this happened so that what is written in their law would be true: 'They hated me for no reason'.[30]

[26]"I will send you the Helper[29] from the Father. He is the Spirit of truth who comes from the Father. When he comes, he will tell about me. [27]And you also must tell people about me because you have been with me from the beginning.

16 "I have told you these things to keep you from giving up. [2]People will put you out of their synagogues.[d] Yes, the time is coming when whoever kills you will think that he is offering service to God. [3]They will do this because they have not known the Father and they have not known me. [4]I have told you these things now. So when the time comes, you will remember that I warned you.

The Work of the Holy Spirit

"I did not tell you these things at the beginning, because I was with you then. [5]Now I am going back to the One who sent me. But none of you asks me, 'Where are you going?' [6]Your hearts are filled with sadness because I have told you these things. [7]But I tell you the truth. It is better for you that I go away. When I go away I will send the Helper[29] to you. If I do not go away, then the Helper will not come. [8]When the Helper comes, he will prove to the people of the world the truth about sin, about being right with God, and about judgement. [9]He will prove to them about sin, because they don't believe in me. [10]He will prove to them that I am right with God, because I am going to the Father. You will not see me any more. [11]And the Helper will prove to them the truth about judgement, because the ruler of this world is already judged.

[12]"I have many more things to say to you, but they are too much for you now. [13]But when the Spirit[d] of truth comes he will lead you into all truth. He will not speak his own words. He will speak only what he hears and will tell you what is to come. [14]The Spirit of truth will bring glory to me. He will take what I have to say and tell it to you. [15]All that the Father has is mine. That is why I said that the Spirit will take what I have to say and tell it to you.

Sadness Will Become Happiness

[16]"After a little while you will not see me. And then after a little while you will see me again."

[17]Some of the followers said to each other, "What does Jesus mean when he says, 'After a little while you will not see me, and then after a little while you will see

me again'? And what does he mean when he says, 'Because I am going to the Father'?" [18]They also asked, "What does he mean by 'a little while'? We don't understand what he is saying."

[19]Jesus saw that the followers wanted to ask him about this. So Jesus said to the followers, "Are you asking each other what I meant when I said, 'After a little while you will not see me. And then after a little while you will see me again'? [20]I tell you the truth. You will cry and be sad, but the world will be happy. You will be sad, but your sadness will become joy. [21]When a woman gives birth to a baby, she has a pain, because her time has come. But when her baby is born, she forgets the pain. She forgets because she is so happy that a child has been born into the world. [22] It is the same with you. Now you are sad. But I will see you again and you will be happy. And no one will take away your joy. [23]In that day you will not ask me for anything. I tell you the truth. My Father will give you anything you ask for in my name. [24]You have never asked for anything in my name. Ask and you will receive. And your joy will be the fullest joy.

Victory over the World

[25]"I have told you these things, using words that hide the meaning. But the time will come when I will not use words like that to tell you things. I will speak to you in plain words about the Father. [26]In that day you will ask the Father for things in my name. I am saying that I will not need to ask the Father for you. [27]No! The Father himself loves you. He loves you because you have loved

me. And he loves you because you have believed that I came from God. [28]I came from the Father into the world. Now I am leaving the world and going back to the Father."

[29]Then the followers of Jesus said, "You are speaking clearly to us now. You are not using words that are hard to understand. [30]We can see now that you know all things. You can answer a person's question even before he asks it. This makes us believe that you came from God."

[31]Jesus answered, "So now you believe? [32]Listen to me. A time is coming when you will be scattered. Each of you will be scattered to his own home. That time is now here. You will leave me. I will be alone. But I am never really alone. Why? Because the Father is with me.

[33]"I told you these things so that you can have peace in me. In this world you will have trouble. But be brave! I have defeated the world!"

Jesus Prays for His Followers

17 After Jesus said these things he looked towards heaven. Jesus prayed, "Father, the time has come. Give glory to your Son so that the Son can give glory to you. [2]You gave the Son power over all people so that the Son could give eternal life to all those people you have given to him. [3]And this is eternal life: that men can know you, the only true God, and that men can know Jesus Christ, the One you sent. [4]I have finished the work you gave me to do. I have brought you glory on earth. [5]And now, Father, give me glory with you. Give me the glory I had with you before the world was made.

[6]"You gave me some men from the world. I have

shown them what you are like. Those men belonged to you, and you gave them to me. They have obeyed your teaching. [7]Now they know that everything you gave me comes from you. [8]I gave these men the teachings that you gave me. They accepted those teachings. They know that I truly came from you. [9]I pray for them now. I am not praying for the people in the world. But I am praying for those men you gave me, because they are yours. [10]All I have is yours, and all you have is mine. And my glory is shown through these men. [11]Now I am coming to you. I will not stay in the world now. But these men are still in the world. Holy Father, keep them safe. Keep them safe by the power of your name (the name you gave me), so that they will be one, the same as you and I are one. [12]While I was with them, I kept them safe. I kept them safe by the power of your name – the name you gave me. I protected them. And only one of them, the one who is going to hell, was lost. He was lost so that what was said in the Scripture[d] would happen.

[13]"I am coming to you now. But I pray these things while I am still in the world. I say these things so that these men can have my joy. I want them to have all of my joy. [14]I have given them your teaching. And the world has hated them. The world hated these men, because they don't belong to the world, just as I don't belong to the world. [15]I am not asking you to take them out of the world. But I am asking that you keep them safe from the Evil One. [16]They don't belong to the world, just as I don't belong to the world. [17]Make them ready for your service through your truth. Your teaching is truth. [18]I have sent

them into the world, just as you sent me into the world. [19]I am making myself ready to serve. I do this for them so that they can truly be ready for your service.

[20]"I pray for these men. But I am also praying for all people who will believe in me because of the teaching of these men. [21]Father, I pray that all people who believe in me can be one. You are in me and I am in you. I pray that these people can also be one in us, so that the world will believe that you sent me. [22]I have given these people the glory that you gave me. I gave them this glory so that they can be one, just as you and I are one. [23]I will be in them and you will be in me. So they will be completely one. Then the world will know that you sent me. And the world will know that you loved these people just as you loved me.

[24]"Father, I want those you have given me to be with me in every place I am. I want them to see my glory. This is the glory you gave me because you loved me before the world was made. [25]Father, you are the One who is good. The world does not know you, but I know you. And these people know that you sent me. [26]I showed them what you are like. And again I will show them what you are like. Then they will have the same love that you have for me. And I will live in them."

Jesus Is Arrested

18 When Jesus finished praying, he left with his followers. They went across the Kidron Valley. On the other side there was a garden of olive trees. Jesus and his followers went there.

[2]Judas knew where this place was, because Jesus met there often with his followers. Judas was the one who turned against Jesus. [3]So Judas led a group of soldiers to the garden. Judas also brought some guards from the leading priests and the Pharisees.[d] They were carrying torches, lanterns, and weapons.

[4]Jesus knew everything that would happen to him. Jesus went out and asked, "Who is it you are looking for?"

[5]The men answered, "Jesus from Nazareth."

Jesus said, "I am Jesus." (Judas, the one who turned against Jesus, was standing there with them.) [6]When Jesus said, "I am Jesus," the men moved back and fell to the ground.

[7]Jesus asked them again, "Who is it you are looking for?"

They said, "Jesus of Nazareth."

[8]Jesus said, "I told you that I am he. So if you are looking for me, then let these other men go." [9]This happened so that the words Jesus said before might come true: "I have not lost any of the men you gave me."

[10]Simon Peter had a sword. He took out the sword and struck the servant of the high priest, cutting off his right ear. (The servant's name was Malchus.) [11]Jesus said to Peter, "Put your sword back. Shall I not drink of the cup[31] the Father has given me?"

Jesus Is Brought Before Annas

[12]Then the soldiers with their commander and the Jewish guards arrested Jesus. They tied him [13]and led

him first to Annas. Annas was the father-in-law of Caiaphas, the high priest that year. [14]Caiaphas was the one who had told the Jews that it would be better if one man died for all the people.

Peter Says He Doesn't Know Jesus

[15]Simon Peter and another one of Jesus' followers went along after Jesus. This follower knew the high priest. So he went with Jesus into the high priest's courtyard. [16]But Peter waited outside near the door. The follower who knew the high priest came back outside. He spoke to the girl at the door and brought Peter inside. [17]The girl at the door said to Peter, "Aren't you also one of that man's followers?"

Peter answered, "No, I am not!"

[18]It was cold, so the servants and guards had built a fire. They were standing around it and warming themselves. Peter was standing with them, warming himself.

The High Priest Questions Jesus

[19]The high priest asked Jesus questions about his followers and his teaching. [20]Jesus answered, "I have spoken openly to everyone. I have always taught in synagogues[d] and in the Temple,[d] where all the Jews come together. I never said anything in secret. [21]So why do you question me? Ask the people who heard my teaching. They know what I said."

[22]When Jesus said this, one of the guards standing there hit him. The guard said, "Is that the way you answer the high priest?"

[23]Jesus answered him, "If I said something wrong, then say what was wrong. But if what I said is true, why do you hit me?"

[24]Then Annas sent Jesus to Caiaphas, the high priest. Jesus was still tied.

Peter Says Again He Doesn't Know Jesus

[25]Simon Peter was standing and warming himself. They said to him, "Aren't you one of that man's followers?"

Peter denied it and said, "No, I am not."

[26]One of the servants of the high priest was there. This servant was a relative of the man whose ear Peter had cut off. The servant said, "Didn't I see you with him in the garden?"

[27]Again Peter said it wasn't true. Just then a cockerel crowed.

Jesus Is Brought Before Pilate

[28]Then the Jews led Jesus from Caiaphas' house to the Roman governor's palace. It was early in the morning. The Jews would not go inside the palace. They did not want to make themselves unclean,[32] because they wanted to eat the Passover[d] meal. [29]So Pilate went outside to them. He asked, "What charges do you bring against this man?"

[30]They answered, "He is a criminal. That is why we brought him to you."

[31]Pilate said to the Jews, "Take him yourselves and judge him by your own law."

They answered, "But we are not allowed to put anyone to death." [32](This happened so that what Jesus had said about how he would die would come true.)

[33]Then Pilate went back inside the palace. He called Jesus to him and asked, "Are you the king of the Jews?"

[34]Jesus said, "Is that your own question, or did others tell you about me?"

[35]Pilate answered, "I am not a Jew. It was your own people and their leading priests who brought you before me. What have you done wrong?"

[36]Jesus said, "My kingdom does not belong to this world. If it belonged to this world, my servants would fight so that I would not be given over to the Jews. But my kingdom is from another place."

[37]Pilate said, "So you are a king!"

Jesus answered, "You say that I am a king. That is true. I was born for this: to tell people about the truth. That is why I came into the world. And everyone who belongs to the truth listens to me."

[38]Pilate said, "What is truth?" After he said this, he went out to the Jews again. He said to them, "I can find nothing to charge against this man. [39]But it is your custom that I free one prisoner to you at the time of the Passover. Do you want me to free this 'King of the Jews'?"

[40]They shouted back, "No, not him! Let Barabbas go free!" (Barabbas was a robber.)

19 Then Pilate ordered that Jesus be taken away and whipped. [2]The soldiers used some thorny branches to make a crown. They put this crown on Jesus'

head and put a purple robe around him. [3]Then they came to Jesus many times and said, "Hail, King of the Jews!" They hit Jesus in the face.

[4]Again Pilate came out and said to the Jews, "Look! I am bringing Jesus out to you. I want you to know that I find nothing I can charge against him." [5]Then Jesus came out, wearing the crown of thorns and the purple robe. Pilate said to the Jews, "Here is the man!"

[6]When the leading priests and the Jewish guards saw Jesus they shouted, "Kill him on a cross! Kill him on a cross!"

But Pilate answered, "Take him and nail him to a cross yourselves. I find nothing I can charge against him."

[7]The Jews answered, "We have a law that says he should die, because he said he is the Son of God."

[8]When Pilate heard this, he was even more afraid. [9]He went back inside the palace and asked Jesus, "Where are you from?" But Jesus did not answer him. [10]Pilate said, "You refuse to speak to me? Don't you know that I have power to set you free and power to have you killed on a cross?"

[11]Jesus answered, "The only power you have over me is the power given to you by God. The man who gave me to you is guilty of a greater sin."

[12]After this, Pilate tried to let Jesus go free. But the Jews cried out, "Anyone who makes himself king is against Caesar. If you let this man go free, you are not Caesar's friend."

[13]Pilate heard what the Jews were saying. So he brought Jesus out to the place called The Stone

Pavement. (In the Jewish language[14] the name is Gabbatha.) Pilate sat down on the judge's seat there. 14It was about six o'clock in the morning on Preparation[d] Day of Passover[d] week. Pilate said to the Jews, "Here is your king!"

15The Jews shouted, "Take him away! Take him away! Kill him on a cross!"

Pilate asked them, "Do you want me to kill your king on a cross?"

The leading priests answered, "The only king we have is Caesar!"

16So Pilate gave Jesus to them to be killed on a cross.

Jesus Is Killed on a Cross

The soldiers took charge of Jesus. 17Carrying his own cross, Jesus went out to a place called The Place of the Skull. (In the Jewish language[14] this place is called Golgotha.) 18There they nailed Jesus to the cross. They also put two other men on crosses, one on each side of Jesus with Jesus in the middle. 19Pilate wrote a sign and put it on the cross. It read: "JESUS OF NAZARETH, THE KING OF THE JEWS." 20The sign was written in the Jewish language, in Latin, and in Greek. Many of the Jews read the sign, because this place where they killed Jesus was near the city. 21The leading Jewish priests said to Pilate, "Don't write, 'The King of the Jews'. But write, 'This man said, I am the King of the Jews'."

22Pilate answered, "What I have written, I have written!"

23After the soldiers nailed Jesus to the cross, they

took his clothes. They divided them into four parts. Each soldier got one part. They also took his long shirt. It was all one piece of cloth, woven from top to bottom. 24So the soldiers said to each other, "We should not tear this into parts. We should throw lots[d] to see who will get it." This happened to give full meaning to the Scripture:[d]

> "They divided my clothes among them.
> And they threw lots[d] for my clothing."
>
> *Psalm* 22:18

So the soldiers did this.

25Jesus' mother stood near his cross. His mother's sister was also standing there, with Mary the wife of Clopas, and Mary Magdalene. 26Jesus saw his mother. He also saw the follower he loved standing there. He said to his mother, "Dear woman, here is your son." 27Then he said to the follower, "Here is your mother." From that time on, this follower took her to live in his home.

Jesus Dies

28After this, Jesus knew that everything had been done. To make the Scripture[d] come true, he said, "I am thirsty."[33] 29There was a jar full of vinegar there, so the soldiers soaked a sponge in it. Then they put the sponge on a branch of a hyssop plant and lifted it to Jesus' mouth. 30Jesus tasted the vinegar. Then he said, "It is finished." He bowed his head and died.

31This day was Preparation[d] Day. The next day was a special Sabbath[d] day. The Jews did not want the bodies to stay on the cross on the Sabbath day. So they asked Pilate to order that the legs of the men be broken[34] and the bodies be taken away. [32]So the soldiers came and broke the legs of the first man on the cross beside Jesus. Then they broke the legs of the man on the other cross beside Jesus. [33]But when the soldiers came to Jesus, they saw that he was already dead. So they did not break his legs, [34]but one of the soldiers stuck his spear into Jesus' side. At once blood and water came out. [35](The one who saw this happen has told about it. The things he says are true. He knows that he tells the truth. He told about it so that you also can believe.) [36]These things happened to make the Scripture come true: "Not one of his bones will be broken."[35] [37]And another Scripture said, "They will look at the one they have stabbed."[36]

Jesus is Buried

[38]Later, a man named Joseph from Arimathea asked Pilate if he could take the body of Jesus. (Joseph was a secret follower of Jesus, because he was afraid of the Jews.) Pilate gave his permission. So Joseph came and took Jesus' body away. [39]Nicodemus went with Joseph. Nicodemus was the man who earlier had come to Jesus at night. He brought about 35 kilograms of spices. This was a mixture of myrrh[d] and aloes.[d] [40]These two men took Jesus' body and wrapped it with the spices in pieces of linen cloth. (This is how the Jews bury people.) [41]In the place where Jesus was killed, there was a garden. In the garden was a new tomb where no one had

ever been buried. [42]The men laid Jesus in that tomb because it was near, and the Jews were preparing to start their Sabbath[d] day.

Jesus' Tomb Is Empty

20 Early on the first day of the week, Mary Magdalene went to the tomb. It was still dark. Mary saw that the large stone had been moved away from the tomb. [2]So Mary ran to Simon Peter and the other follower (the one Jesus loved). Mary said, "They have taken the Lord out of the tomb. We don't know where they have put him."

[3]So Peter and the other follower started for the tomb. [4]They were both running, but the other follower ran faster than Peter. So the other follower reached the tomb first. [5]He bent down and looked in. He saw the strips of linen cloth lying there, but he did not go in. [6]Then following him came Simon Peter. He went into the tomb and saw the strips of linen lying there. [7]He also saw the cloth that had been around Jesus' head. The cloth was folded up and laid in a different place from the strips of linen. [8]Then the other follower, who had reached the tomb first, also went in. He saw and believed. [9](These followers did not yet understand from the Scriptures[d] that Jesus must rise from death.)

Jesus Appears to Mary Magdalene

[10]Then the followers went back home. [11]But Mary stood outside the tomb, crying. While she was still crying, she bent down and looked inside the tomb.

[12]She saw two angels dressed in white. They were sitting where Jesus' body had been, one at the head and one at the feet.

[13]They asked her, "Woman, why are you crying?"

She answered, "They have taken away my Lord. I don't know where they have put him." [14]When Mary said this, she turned around and saw Jesus standing there. But she did not know that it was Jesus.

[15]Jesus asked her, "Woman, why are you crying? Whom are you looking for?"

Mary thought he was the gardener. So she said to him, "Did you take him away, sir? Tell me where you put him, and I will get him."

[16]Jesus said to her, "Mary."

Mary turned toward Jesus and said in the Jewish language,[14] "Rabboni." (This means Teacher.)

[17]Jesus said to her, "Don't hold me. I have not yet gone up to the Father. But go to my brothers and tell them this: 'I am going back to my Father and your Father. I am going back to my God and your God'."

[18]Mary Magdalene went and said to the followers, "I have seen the Lord!" And she told them what Jesus had said to her.

Jesus Appears to His Followers

[19]It was the first day of the week. That evening the followers were together. The doors were locked, because they were afraid of the Jews. Then Jesus came and stood among them. He said, "Peace be with you!" [20]After he said this, he showed them his hands and his

side. The followers were very happy when they saw the Lord.

[21]Then Jesus said again, "Peace be with you! As the Father sent me, I now send you." [22]After he said this, he breathed on them and said, "Receive the Holy Spirit.[d] [23]If you forgive anyone his sins, they are forgiven. If you don't forgive them, they are not forgiven."

Jesus Appears to Thomas

[24]Thomas (called Didymus) was not with the followers when Jesus came. Thomas was one of the 12. [25]The other followers told Thomas, "We have seen the Lord."

But Thomas said, "I will not believe it until I see the nail marks in his hands. And I will not believe until I put my finger where the nails were and put my hand into his side."

[26]A week later the followers were in the house again. Thomas was with them. The doors were locked, but Jesus came in and stood among them. He said, "Peace be with you!" [27]Then he said to Thomas, "Put your finger here. Look at my hands. Put your hand here in my side. Stop doubting and believe."

[28]Thomas said to him, "My Lord and my God!"

[29]Then Jesus told him, "You believe because you see me. Those who believe without seeing me will be truly happy."

Why John Wrote This Book

[30]Jesus did many other miracles[d] in front of his followers that are not written in this book. [31]But these are written so that you can believe that Jesus is the Christ,[d]

the Son of God. Then, by believing, you can have life through his name.

Jesus Appears to Seven Followers

21 Later, Jesus showed himself to his followers by Lake Galilee.[37] This is how it happened. [2]Some of the followers were together. They were Simon Peter, Thomas (called Didymus), Nathanael from Cana in Galilee, the two sons of Zebedee, and two other followers. [3]Simon Peter said, "I am going out to fish."

The other followers said, "We will go with you." So they went out and got into the boat. They fished that night but caught nothing.

[4]Early the next morning Jesus stood on the shore. But the followers did not know that it was Jesus. [5]Then he said to them, "Friends, have you caught any fish?"

They answered, "No".

[6]He said, "Throw your net into the water on the right side of the boat, and you will find some." So they did this. They caught so many fish that they could not pull the net back into the boat.

[7]The follower whom Jesus loved said to Peter, "It is the Lord!" When Peter heard him say this, he wrapped his coat around himself. (Peter had taken his clothes off.) Then he jumped into the water. [8]The other followers went to shore in the boat, dragging the net full of fish. They were not very far from shore, only about 100 metres. [9]When the followers stepped out of the boat and onto the shore, they saw a fire of hot coals. There were fish on the fire, and there was bread.

[10]Then Jesus said, "Bring some of the fish that you caught."

[11]Simon Peter went into the boat and pulled the net to the shore. It was full of big fish. There were 153. Even though there were so many, the net did not tear. [12]Jesus said to them, "Come and eat." None of the followers dared ask him, "Who are you?" They knew it was the Lord. [13]Jesus came and took the bread and gave it to them. He also gave them the fish.

[14]This was now the third time that Jesus showed himself to his followers after he was raised from death.

Jesus Talks to Peter

[15]When they had finished eating, Jesus said to Simon Peter, "Simon, son of John, do you love me more than these?"

He answered, "Yes, Lord, you know that I love you."

Jesus said, "Take care of my lambs."

[16]Again Jesus said, "Simon, son of John, do you love me?"

He answered, "Yes, Lord, you know that I love you."

Jesus said, "Take care of my sheep."

[17] A third time he said, "Simon, son of John, do you love me?"

Peter was hurt because Jesus asked him the third time, "Do you love me?" Peter said, "Lord, you know everything. You know that I love you!"

He said to him, "Take care of my sheep. [18]I tell you the truth. When you were younger, you tied your own belt and went where you wanted. But when you are old, you will put out your hands and someone else will tie them. They will take you where you don't want to go." [19](Jesus said this to show how Peter would die to give glory to God.) Then Jesus said to Peter, "Follow me!"

[20]Peter turned and saw that the follower Jesus loved was walking behind them. (This was the follower who had leaned against Jesus at the supper and had said, "Lord, who will turn against you?") [21]When Peter saw him behind them he asked Jesus, "Lord, what about him?"

[22]Jesus answered, "Perhaps I want him to live until I come back. That should not be important to you. You follow me!"

[23]So a story spread among the brothers that this follower would not die. But Jesus did not say that he would not die. He only said, "Perhaps I want him to live until I come back. That should not be important to you."

[24]That follower is the one who is telling these things. He is the one who has now written them down. We know that what he says is true.

[25]There are many other things that Jesus did. If every one of them were written down, I think the whole world would not be big enough for all the books that would be written.

Notes

[1] The Greek word is "logos", meaning any kind of communication. It could be translated "message". Here, it means Christ. Christ was the way God told people about himself.

[2] John the Baptist, who preached to people about Christ's coming (Matthew 3, Luke 3).

[3] This could be translated, "but the only God is very close to the Father." Also, some Greek copies say, "but the only Son is very close to the Father."

[4] A man who spoke for God. He lived hundreds of years before Christ.

[5] They probably meant the prophet that God told Moses he would send (Deuteronomy 18:15-19).

[6] Name for Jesus. Jesus is like the lambs that were offered as a sacrifice to God.

[7] The Greek name "Peter", like the Aramaic name "Cephas", means "rock".

[8] These words are from Genesis 28:12.

[9] The Jews washed themselves in special ways before eating, before worshipping in the Temple, and at other special times.

[10] Quotation from Psalm 69:9.

[11] The people of Israel were dying from snake bites. God told Moses to put a brass snake on a pole. The people who looked at the snake were healed (Numbers 21:4-9).

[12] This can also be translated "Jews don't use things that Samaritans have used".

[13] As a farmer sends workers to harvest grain, Jesus sends his followers out to bring people to God.

[14] Aramaic, the language of the Jews in the first century.

[15] Also called Bethsaida or Bethzatha, a pool of water north of the Temple in Jerusalem.

[16] Some Greek copies add "and they waited for the water to move". A few later copies add verse 4: "Sometimes an angel of the Lord came down to the pool

and stirred up the water. After the angel did this, the first person to go into the pool was healed of any sickness he had."

[17] Quotation from Psalm 78:24.

[18] Quotation from Isaiah 54:13.

[19] Moses gave God's people the law that God gave him on Mount Sinai (Exodus 34:29-32).

[20] The story about Nicodemus going and talking to Jesus is in John 3:1-21.

[21] Some early Greek manuscripts do not contain 7:53–8:11.

[22] Jesus is talking about people who are spiritually blind, not physically blind.

[23] Quotation from Psalm 82:6.

[24] Being raised from death to live again.

[25] One coin, a denarius, was the average pay for one day's work.

[26] Literally, "Hosanna", a Hebrew word used at first in praying to God for help, but at this time it was probably a shout of joy used in praising God or his Messiah.

[27] Quotation from Psalm 41:9.

[28] Literally, "lying". The people of that time ate lying down and leaning on one arm.

[29] "Counsellor", or "Comforter". Jesus is talking about the Holy Spirit.

[30] These words could be from Psalm 35:19 or Psalm 69:4.

[31] Jesus is talking about the bad things that will happen to him. Accepting these things will be very hard, like drinking a cup of something that tastes very bitter.

[32] Going into a non-Jewish place would make them unfit to eat the Passover Feast, according to Jewish law.

[33] Read Psalms 22:15, 69:21.

[34] The breaking of the men's bones would make them die sooner.

[35] Quotation from Psalm 34:20. The idea is from Exodus 12:46; Numbers 9:12.

[36] Quotation from Zechariah 12:10.

[37] Literally, "Sea of Tiberias".

Dictionary

Adultery (ah-DUL-ter-ee) is breaking a marriage promise by having sexual relations with someone other than your husband or wife. (Exodus 20:14; Mark 10:11,12; John 8:3–5)

Aloes (AL-ohs) were oils from sweet-smelling sap of certain trees. They were used for perfume, medicine and to prepare bodies for burial. (Numbers 24:6; John 19:39)

Christ (KRYST) means "anointed (or chosen) one" in Greek. In Hebrew the word is "Messiah". Jesus is the Christ. He was chosen by God to save people from their sins. (Mark 8:29; 14:61,62; Luke 23:2; Acts 2:36; 17:3; 18:28)

Circumcision (SIR-kum-SIH-zhun) This means to cut off the foreskin of the male sex organ. Each Jewish baby boy was circumcised on the eighth day after he was born. This act was done as a sign of the agreement God had made with his people, the Jews. Because of this, the Jews sometimes are called "the circumcision" and non-Jews are called "the uncircumcision". (Leviticus 12:3; John 7:22; Acts 7:8)

Clean is used to describe the state of a person, animal or action that is pleasing to God. God called some animals clean and said they could be eaten. People who had not touched or eaten anything God said was unclean were called clean. Or, if they did not have a disease that made them unclean, they were called clean. They could live and serve God normally. (Genesis 7:2; Leviticus 20:25; Deuteronomy 14:3–20).

Demon (DEE-mun) was an evil spirit from the devil. Sometimes a demon lived in a person. But Jesus has more power than demons and could make them come out of people. (Deuteronomy 32:17; Psalm 106:37; Matthew 12:22; Luke 8:26–39)

Feast of Dedication was an eight-day celebration for the Jews. It was a way of being thankful that the Temple had been cleansed again. This was done in 164 B.C. after the Greeks had spoiled and ruined it. The celebration is called Hanukkah today by the Jews. (John 10:22)

Feast of Shelters is also called the Feast of Booths or Feast of Tabernacles. The people gathered fruit and lived in tent-like shelters for a week. This feast reminded them of how God had taken care of them when the Israelites left Egypt and lived in tents in the wilderness. (Exodus 23:14–17; Deuteronomy 16:13–17)

Holy Spirit (HO-lee SPIH-rit) is one of the three persons of God. The other two persons are God the Father and God the Son (Jesus). The Holy Spirit helped the apostles do miracles. He led men to write God's word. The Holy Spirit lives in Christians today. He is also called the Spirit of Christ, the Spirit of God, and the Comforter. (Genesis 1:2; John 3:5–8; 16:13; Acts 2:1–4; 5:32; Romans 5:5; 8:9–16; 2 Peter 1:20,21)

Lots were sticks, stones or pieces of bone thrown like dice to decide something. Often God controlled the result of the lots to let the people know what he wanted them to do. (Numbers 26:55,56; Proverbs 18:18; Jonah 1:7; Luke 1:9; 23:34; Acts 1:26)

Manna (MAN-ah) means "what is it?" It was the white, sweet-tasting food God gave the people of Israel in the wilderness. It appeared on the ground during the night so they could gather it in the morning. (Exodus 16:13–35; Numbers 11:7–9; Joshua 5:12; Hebrews 9:4)

Miracle (MYR-ih-k'l) is a Latin word that means "wonderful thing". It is a great event which can be done only by God's help. Miracles are special signs to show God's power. In the Old Testament God used miracles to rescue his people. Jesus did miracles to prove that he was God's Son. The Bible tells us of many miracles. The sick were healed, the blind were given sight, the crippled were able to walk and people could speak languages they had never studied. Sometimes people were even brought back to life after they had died. The best miracle was Jesus' coming back to life after he was killed on the cross. (Nehemiah 9:17; Psalm 77:11,14; Matthew 28:5–7; Luke 23:8; John 2:1–11; 3:2; 20:30,31; Acts 4:16–22; 8:13)

Mount of Olives is a hill covered with olive trees near Jerusalem. The garden of Gethsemane is on one side of the Mount of Olives. Jesus was praying there when the Roman soldiers came to arrest him. Some of the same olive trees that were in the garden when Jesus was on earth may still be there today. (2 Samuel 15:30; Luke 22:39–52; Acts 1:12)

Myrrh (MUR) was a sweet-smelling liquid taken from certain trees and shrubs. It was used as a perfume and as a pain reliever. It was one of the gifts the wise men gave Jesus when he was born. (Genesis 37:25; 43:11; Proverbs 7:17; Matthew 2:11; Mark 15:23; John 19:39)

Nard was an expensive perfume. It was expensive because it had to be imported from India. (Song of Solomon 4:13; Mark 14:3; John 12:3)

Passover Feast (PASS-o-ver FEEST) was an important holy day for the Jews in the spring of each year. They ate a special meal on this day to remind them that God had freed them from being slaves in Egypt. Jesus was killed at Passover time. (Exodus 12:27; Numbers 9; Joshua 5:10; Matthew 26:2,17–19)

Pharisees (FA-rih-seez) means "the separate people". They were a Jewish religious group who followed the religious laws and customs very strictly. Jesus often spoke against the Pharisees for their religious teachings and traditions. Many of the Pharisees did not like Jesus because he did not follow all of their rules. (Matthew 5:20; 23:23–36; Mark 7:1–13; Luke 18:9–14)

Preparation Day (prep-a-RAY-shun DAY) was the day before the Sabbath day. On that day the Jews prepared or got everything ready for the Sabbath. (Luke 23:54; John 19:14,31)

Prophesy (PROH-fes-sy) is to speak a prophecy, which means "message". A prophecy is God speaking through chosen people called prophets. The Old Testament has many prophecies about the Saviour who was to come into the world. Jesus was the answer to these prophecies. (Ezekiel 12:26–28; 2 Peter 1:20,21; Revelation 22:18,19) See "prophet".

Prophet (PROH-fet) means "messenger" or one who speaks for someone else. With God's help, a prophet was able to tell the people God's message correctly.

Sometimes prophets told what would happen in the future. A woman who spoke God's message was called a prophetess (2 Kings 22:14; Luke 2:36). Several books of the Old Testament were written by prophets, including Jeremiah, Amos, Jonah and Micah. (2 Kings 6:12–16; 17:12–13; Matthew 2:5,6; Luke 16:29–31; 24; 25–27; Romans 1:2; 1 Corinthians 12:28,29; 1 Peter 1:10–12)

Sabbath (SAB-uth) means "rest". It was the seventh day of the Jewish week, their day of worship to God. The Jews were not allowed to work on this day. Some Jews became angry with Jesus because he healed people on the Sabbath. They thought this was breaking the Old Testament law of the Sabbath. (Exodus 16:23–30; 20:8–11; Matthew 12:9–14; Luke 6:1–11; Acts 18:4; Colossians 2:16,17)

Samaritan (suh-MAR-ih-t'n) was a person from the area of Samaria in Palestine. Samaria was between Galilee and Judea. These people were only part Jewish, so the Jews did not accept them. They hated the Samaritans. But Jesus showed love and concern for the Samaritans. One story that Jesus told is known as the story of "the good Samaritan". (Luke 10:30–37; John 4:1–42)

Scriptures (SCRIP-churs) means "writings". They are the special writings of God's word for man. When the word Scriptures is used in the New Testament, it usually means the Old Testament. Later, it came to mean the whole Bible. (Daniel 9:2; Luke 24:27,32,45; Acts 8:32–35; 17:2,11; 2 Timothy 3:16; 2 Peter 1:20; 3:16).

Solomon's Porch (SOL-o-mon's PORCH) was a covered courtyard on the east side of the Temple. People gathered here to sell animals and exchange money. Others met to discuss the Law of Moses. (1 Kings 7:6; John 10:23; Acts 3:11; 5:12)

Son of Man was a name Jesus called himself. It showed that he was God's Son, but he was also a man. This title for Jesus comes from "one who looked like a human being" in Daniel 7:13–14. There Daniel prophesies about Jesus. (Matthew 24:30; 26:64; Mark 13:26; 14:62; Luke 21:27; 22:69)

Synagogue (SIN-uh-gog) is a Greek word that means "a meeting". By the first century, the Jews met in synagogues to read and study the Scriptures. The building was also used as the Jewish court and as a school. Both Jesus and Paul often went to the Jewish synagogues to teach and discuss the Scriptures. (Matthew 4:23; Luke 4:16,17; Acts 15:21; 17:1,10)

Temple (TEM-p'l) is a building where people worship their gods. God told the Jewish people to worship him at the Temple in Jerusalem. This temple had been built by King Solomon. It was later destroyed by the Babylonians. It was rebuilt by Zerubbabel. This Temple was destroyed by a Roman general, Pompey. Herod built a third Temple which was used in Jesus' time. (2 Chronicles 2–7; Ezra 3:10–12; Mark 11:15–17; Acts 7:47; 19:27)

The New Testament also speaks of a Christian's body as a temple. That is because God's Spirit lives in the Christian. (Acts 7:48; 19:27; 1 Corinthians 6:19)